There Are No Alligators in Heaven!

*A family's perspectives
on surviving the
unrelenting savagery
of Cystic Fibrosis*

by
Jennifer Hale
and her parents
Donna & Evan Michael Codell

Jennifer Hale, Donna & Evan Michael Codell

There Are No Alligators in Heaven!

A family's perspectives on surviving the unrelenting savagery of Cystic Fibrosis

2017 / 224 pp / 15 photographs
Starshine Galaxy Foundation NFP / Geneva, Illinois
ISBN13: 978-0-9908547-2-2 / ISBN10: 0-9908547-2-8
Library of Congress Control Number (LCCN): 2017941930

Book Design & Development Services provided by Rod Mebane and Angela Scaperlanda Buján
Cover Design Services provided by Aurelie Krauss

We are grateful to Emily Schaller and the Rock CF Foundation (letsrockcf.org) for their generous financial support.

There Are No Alligators in Heaven! is published by Starshine Galaxy Foundation NFP – a private nonprofit organization based in Geneva, Illinois. For all matters related to *There Are No Alligators in Heaven!* contact:

starmaster@starshinegalaxy.org.

*We have all known individuals
in very difficult circumstances, perhaps
with a terminal illness or a severe
physical handicap, who maintain
magnificent emotional strength.*

How inspired we are by their integrity!

*Nothing has a greater, longer-lasting
impression upon another person than
the awareness that someone has
transcended suffering, has transcended
circumstance, and is embodying and
expressing a value that inspires and
ennobles and lifts life.*

— Steven R. Covey, *Seven Habits of Highly
Effective People*

Contents

About this Book

Donna and Evan Codell had a powerful story to tell – one that they felt would make an important difference to others. The story is about their daughter, Jennifer, who was an amazing example of how to live fully in spite of the unrelenting savagery of Cystic Fibrosis, which eventually claimed her life in December 2015 at the age of 43.

In the middle of 2016, however, the Codells became increasingly concerned that they would not be able to tell their story. Their concern was based on two things: 1) Neither of the Codells had much experience writing. So, despite workshops on authoring books and other efforts at skill-building, they were challenged to get the right words on paper. 2) They were running out of time. Four years prior, Evan had been diagnosed with Stage 4 lung cancer and was given about 6 months to live. Now, four years later, after having lived well beyond his prognosis, Evan's decline was evident.

By chance, Donna met Angela Scaperlanda Buján and, as Angela learned about the Codells' predicament, she mentioned that Starshine Galaxy Foundation – a nonprofit organization that she works with – is focused on publishing stories by and about children who have passed away. Connections were made, and an alliance was formed. Rod Mebane, the Foundation's managing director, joined the team and, given the Codells' challenges, they committed to a strategy of deep, structured interviews that would create a transcript to serve as the textual foundation for their book – the one that you are now holding.

In total, we conducted 2½ days of recorded interviews, staged in 3 sessions in late 2016. We held the last session on Monday, December 12. Two days later, on Wednesday, December 14, Evan Codell passed away. Although Evan did not live to see the finished work, he died knowing that he gave it his all and that their story would indeed be told.

Although the story unfolds conversationally between her parents, Jennifer's own voice is integral throughout the book. As you read *There Are No Alligators in Heaven!* you will see that Jennifer's words, creations, and images help frame the book from beginning to end – starting with the *Introduction.*

In the latter phases of her life, Jennifer had been active in networking with other adult survivors of cystic fibrosis and published numerous articles for CF Roundtable, the publication of the US Adult CF Association, Inc., (USACFA). In addition, many of Jen's excerpts throughout the book were taken from her articles in *CF Roundtable.* With the generous permission of *CF Roundtable,* we are including a complete collection of her inspiring articles in one location.

This book project initially began to help the Codells tell the story of Jennifer – a courageous, positive, loving, happy child, who against the odds grew into a beautiful, strong woman and lived fully and purposefully, but was still taken too soon. The project quickly evolved into something much deeper. In an ironic twist of fate, Evan was visibly walking his own "journey" while developing this book. He was experiencing firsthand so many of the horrific effects of lung disease that Jennifer battled her entire life, and he now understood more profoundly just how strong and courageous their daughter really was.

Another individual who knows the depth of Jennifer's strength and courage is Mark Hale – Jennifer's husband and, in her words, her "rock" and her "everything." In publishing *There Are No Alligators in Heaven!* we would like to thank Mark for his support during the project.

Against this backdrop, here is the Codells' story of Jennifer – in their words and hers – to inspire hope and confidence in others. On a personal level, it was an honor to be invited to hear this family's firsthand account of their perilous, yet joyful journey together through not one, but two terminal illnesses, and it is our privilege to offer the family's story to you. There may be additional information of interest to you on the authors' website: noalligatorsinheaven.com.

Please feel encouraged to share your reactions to *There Are No Alligators in Heaven!* by contacting the publisher at: starmaster@starshinegalaxy.org.

Respectfully,

Rod Mebane   Angela Scaperlanda Buján

STARSHINE GALAXY FOUNDATION NFP
GENEVA, ILLINOIS

Dedication

I'd like to dedicate this book to my courageous daughter, Jennifer, and her father, Evan Michael Codell. They both put up a good fight and will always be remembered as shining spirits!

— Donna Codell

INTRODUCTION

by Jennifer Codell, Age 10½ (in 1983)

Jennifer Codell (My Life)
I have C.F. but I am still the
same. I learned to cope with it
by my perants who are Mike &
Donna. They helped me alot
by not lying to me and telling
me wuts wrong and not just
saying "oh you don't have anything
and then scaring me. I love them
alot for that! From what I
know about C.F. wich I know
alot it is a lung deasece,
and my musus is harder to
get out because it is thicker
and I have to take Pills
and one of them is pancrea
that helps me dijest my
food and I take it all the
time before every meal but
I don't have to take it in
snacks that I have. If I
don't take it for a long time
I'll start getting skninny.
I whe about 77 or 80 pounds
thats good! I also have
to do exerisizes to get the

~~music~~ mucus out and before
that ~~or~~ I do a breathing
thing and that goes threw
mouth and I such up medicin
It doesn't ~~to~~ take to long
because we been doing it
for 8 years. In school nobody
can tell because I not skinny
and I eat good. Two boys
like me in school, one of
them that I ~~do~~ don't like
gave me a pen. Rachel Lewis
and Lisa know real good about
my C.F. they are my ~~not~~ best
friends. This other girl knows
that I have to take pills
but she doesn't know
much. In school I don't
think anybody ~~notice~~ notice
me but who cares. My family
goes alot with me and they
love me a wholl bunch. I
love I mean love sports and
I play baseball, swim, basketball,
pano, sing, temnis, run and things

I don't really mind having C.F. but there's nothing I could do about it!

yeh I'm HAPPY!

Jennifer Codell

PROLOGUE

By Donna Codell

When I was a little girl I would dream of getting married and having a family filled with children. I was a romantic. I was in love with love. I adored children. I had hopes of a beautiful life with a man that I loved and beautiful children, bringing them up to be good citizens, respectful of others, helpful and loving. I was determined to be good in the things that I loved to do. I was a very competitive, outgoing person who loved life, loved people, and was very social. I was the baby of the family, so everybody "took care of Donna." Everybody was loving to me, so how could I not be loving to other people? That's what I grew up with.

I went to college for a year to get my MRS degree, and successfully became a Mrs. That's just what I wanted. I wasn't aiming to work in a certain profession at that time. My main goal was to have a family. I really didn't have any fears about anything. Having children was so important to me. When Michael and I got married, I said, *We've got to start trying, because it might take a long time.* I pushed him into that. But it didn't take a long time at all. We got pregnant on the first try!

Jennifer was born with 10 fingers and 10 toes, and I thought everything was fine. I had no reason to think otherwise. And, after she was born, I couldn't get enough of her. I must have kissed her a million times a day. She just brought so much joy to me, even with her crying. I loved being a mother to her, taking care of her. You know when you're little and you take care of your dolls? It seems like the same thing to me, but it's a life, and I wanted to make sure that I did the best for this little person. I wanted to take care of her to the best of my knowledge and protect her.

A lot of people get babysitters or give their children to someone else to watch. I never wanted to do that. I wanted to be with her all the time. Just being with her and caring for her was the greatest source of joy. I took such pride in having a child – taking care of a little girl who couldn't take care of herself.

When Jennifer turned two, she started coughing a lot. I was concerned and took her to the doctor, and that's when the process started that led to finding out she had Cystic Fibrosis. When we got that diagnosis, our whole world changed. Here we had a beautiful little girl that was growing, developing, and the doctors are telling us that she has a good chance of dying sooner than she should. You can imagine how your world completely collapses. Now, I had to make sure she doesn't get sick. Make sure I give her medicine. Make sure she's safe in every way that I could keep her safe. When we found out, as shocked as we were, there was no doubt in our minds that, even though they said children with Cystic Fibrosis typically only live to 15, she was going to live longer because I was going to do everything in my power to help her live as long as possible, making sure she got the proper nutrition and care, and to live a normal life as well as she could.

In practically every way, Jennifer was a normal kid. She loved life. She loved to play. She loved to have fun. She loved sports. She loved people just like we did. And she mostly lived a normal childhood. We always had friends in the house. We made it comfortable, and she knew that she could bring anyone home she wanted to – our house was open to anyone. We worked very hard to make sure she wasn't different from any other child other than having a terminal illness.

I always told Jennifer that life is like a poker hand. You get dealt the cards, and you need to do the best you can with the cards you were dealt. Dealing with a child with a terminal disease is different from a healthy child. We used our intuition and common sense to try and make Jennifer's life as normal as possible, with a positive attitude, a smile, and kindness. There are many things you have to do, though, that just aren't normal.

Dealing with adversity made a stronger bond among my husband, daughter, and me because it was us against all odds. Michael, Jennifer, and I were the 3 musketeers. We stood together, we were strong together, and nothing could come between us. We did our best to live life to its fullest and never give up hope.

I believe that we did the very best we could do with the knowledge we had. We made sure we found out everything there was to know and everything there was to do for this disease. We wanted to make sure that we kept Jennifer as healthy as possible in hopes that, during her lifetime, there would be a cure for this devastating disease. That she'd be a candidate for better things coming. We made sure that Jennifer grew up knowing how to take care of herself and to never give up the fight. As Jennifer got older, she also felt a commitment to help others in the CF community by lifting their spirits when they were low and giving encouragement when needed.

Over the years, I would have taken the pain away from Jennifer if I could. Obviously, I couldn't. Raising a child with a terminal illness is a difficult journey, but one that has given me determination, under-standing, and a sense of pride. My daughter, Jennifer, was someone that you'd love to be around. She was a loyal friend, and she was the most courageous person I have ever known. She was my hero, and I always told her that.

To a young couple just starting out with a child who's just been diagnosed with a terminal illness, the most im-portant thing I can say is: Love each other. Love each other with all the love that you can give. Be respectful of each other. Try to take care of yourself as well as the other people in your family. For any family that's just learned that their child has a terminal illness, please get help. Find someone that you can talk to and spill your guts to. Get involved and connect with other people that have the same problems. Do everything in your power to know everything about the disease. Make sure you do every-thing to keep your child as healthy as possible.

Lastly, be positive. Laugh a lot. Live your life to its fullest and never give up hope. Make your child feel safe. I hope reading *There Are No Alligators in Heaven!* will help you do that by offering hope, strength, and uplifting stories, against the backdrop of a very harsh reality.

I must say that writing this book with my husband Michael was very rewarding. It brought us closer together in a very special way at a critical time in our lives. I am so grateful that he was still around to express his thoughts. When my husband was diagnosed in March 2012 with Stage 4 lung cancer, he was given 6 months at most to live. With good wellness practices, chemo treatments, and a fighting spirit, Michael lived until December of 2016.

A word about my husband's name. You see that I just called him "Michael" while elsewhere in the book he is referred to as "Evan." Here's the story: He was born Evan Michael Codell. When he was young, he decided to use his middle name because other kids made fun of him – for his name (Evan) and because he was short and had kinky hair. So, one of the things he did was to change his name – to Michael. That's how it was when I met him, and I've always thought of my husband as Michael or Mike.

After learning about cancer, starting on "the journey" as he referred to it, my husband went through a metamorphosis of sorts. Michael, to him, was gone. The name just didn't seem to fit who he was becoming since knowing he had a terminal illness. He stopped using his middle name, and his given name "Evan" took over for the few years he had left.

He got a lot of strength from Jennifer when he was diagnosed. Even though she was going through bad times herself, she helped him as much as she could with encouraging phone calls, emails, texts, and she gave everything in her power that she could give to him.

I was a nurse to Jennifer, but I had help from Michael. I was a nurse to Michael, too, but I didn't have another person to help me like he helped me with Jennifer, especially after Jennifer passed away in December 2015. For those of you who have never been in this situation, it's scary. It's scary, it's lonely – I can't really explain it, but I had to be strong. I had to stay strong and be there for him, whatever he needed. Helping Michael while he was in hospice, well, it was almost like I relived what I went through with Jennifer. I was strong when I had to be strong, and Michael was strong when he had to be strong.

In this context, writing this book while going through the trauma of Michael's cancer gave us something else to think about and something else to do. In addition, just reliving the wonderful things and obviously the not so wonderful things brought Jennifer alive and brought her back into our family as we talked about her and wrote about her.

I hope our story will encourage you to never give up. It's amazing how strong you can be, one day at a time, when faced with adversity, and you can deal with all of it in a positive light. Life throws many curve balls and, if you choose to face them head on, you will get better each day. I hope you will be inspired by our words and that you find some peace from our story as you navigate through your own trials and tribulations.

1 – A DREAM COME TRUE

Jennifer: I was born a bouncy, vibrant, cuddly baby girl. Perfect in every way with a future so bright, like the song goes, "you gotta wear shades."

Dreams of having a baby

Donna: I wanted to have a baby very badly ...

My husband and I both have fuzzy curly hair and, when she was in my little tummy, we called her "Frizzy" because we didn't think a child would come out with straight hair.

We got married in 1969, and Jennifer was born in 1972. It took her 2 days to come out, very stubborn. I went into the hospital on Thursday, they sent me home on Friday, and I came back on Saturday. Never slept for 2 days. The doctor recorded her birth at 4:44 p.m. She was 5 pound, 5 ounces when she was born. I don't know why it took her so long to come out.

In those days, the husband couldn't come in to the room, so Michael had to wait outside, and it was in January. He was very cold, and he remembers the nurse taking the baby and putting it under the faucet, and he on tippy-toes trying to see if it was a girl or boy.

Evan: After the delivery, the nurse gave Jennifer to Donna to hold, and I literally was uncertain as to what the baby was, so I asked, "What do we got here?"

When I saw that it was a girl, I wasn't shocked. Let's put it this way – I didn't care. I really didn't care. A lot of guys say, "Oh, yeah, I want a son." Well, we all want sons, but in reality who cares? At that time, I thought, "Okay, we have a girl. We're starting with a girl, the next one will be a son," because Donna and I wanted and even talked about having at least 2 to 3 kids. That's what we wanted.

That all being said, it was terribly cold and they weren't too accommodating in the hospital.

Donna: I told my husband to bring a pillow when he picked me up so I could sit on a pillow going home, bringing the baby. Michael brought a pillow and put a trash bag over it. Well, I went home wearing a dress and tights, so needless to say I got in the car and started sliding around the car because of the slick trash bag, so that was funny.

We went home to Evanston and lived in Evanston until Jennifer was 3½.

Evan: We didn't have a name for her right away.

Donna: Well, we were picking ... His father's name was James. Evan lost his father when he was 17, so we were definitely going to name her after his father, using the J. I actually wanted the name Jennifer – I think I did choose it because I knew a girl when I was growing up whose name was Jennifer. She was 3 years older than me, and she was beautiful.

Evan: I don't remember that.

Donna: I never told you. See, there is a surprise.

She was a beautiful girl, and my daughter had to be called Jennifer. Her middle name was Rae – starting with an R for my Grandma Rose ...

Evan: In the Jewish tradition, what you do is you name your children after deceased relatives. (They can't be alive. And there's no juniors.) You use the name or, if it's the opposite gender, you can use the initial.

In general, I have to say that our feelings were no different than other young couples trying to start a family. Our expectations, our hopes, our prayers were not outside the box in any way, shape, or form. Now, we just did what we thought was natural, and wishes and hopes for the baby were again totally normal. Healthy, all the toes and all the fingers were there, other than that ...

We were wishing for the child Jennifer to be healthy, have a fulfilled life – typical of any parent. If you ask them and if they're honest, they would say, "That's all we want from our kids. Healthy and happy." Whatever else comes about, first of all we don't know, and we can't predict, we can hope for, but again I didn't expect anything extraordinary out of Jennifer. Absolutely not, that would be silly and unfair to her, to put that burden on her, if you will.

My baby was beautiful

Donna: Okay, my baby was born. She had 10 fingers, 10 toes. My baby was beautiful. Everything was great.

Evan: Jennifer was a happy kid. Also, and I know every parent says this, but she was beautiful. She looked like the Gerber baby – it was amazing – the big cheeks, sweet smile, all that stuff.

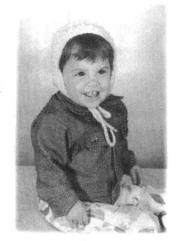

Every parent, and rightly so, should look at their child and say, "This is the best of the best. The most beautiful, the most intelligent, just the best." If you don't do that, there's something wrong with you as a parent, if you don't see that in your baby.

A special child from the beginning

Evan: But, with Jennifer in those early days, she was different. Besides her physical beauty, she had qualities that we didn't see in other children. She was intensely aware of things around her, and she was extremely responsive to stimuli of all sorts. Also, her eyes were penetrating – it was as if she had a special ability to perceive things, although sometimes it felt as though she was looking through you.

Part of it was that our home in those days was filled with things that would stimulate Jennifer, mainly because of Donna. There was very little quiet time. Something was always going on, either intended or not intended. We didn't know what we were doing, we just did things because it made sense. That being said, everything we did from the beginning was focused on

Jennifer, not spoiling her in any way, but focused on her.

I think the approach served us very well. As my mother used to say, the proof is in the pudding. And the result of what we did was Jennifer – there's no better proof than that that we did something right. It came from a combination of instinct and love.

But she seemed to cry a lot

Donna: Although Jennifer was a very happy child, when I first brought her home she cried a lot, and I didn't know what was wrong. So, I fed her because I figured she's hungry. I would feed her every hour and a half because she was crying.

Well, a couple of years later, when she was diagnosed with Cystic Fibrosis, we learned that food goes right through them, and that's why she was always hungry. So, it's a good thing I had a lot of milk.

Evan: This is a great example of how we figured things out in those early years even though we didn't have the knowledge.

Donna: She was also small. She was 5 lb. 5 oz. when she was borne and dropped to 5 lb. 1 oz. when I took her home.

Evan: But we figured she would be small. I mean, let's be honest – Donna and I are not giant people. So, we thought, of course, she's going to be little. Duh.

Donna: Also, the thing was in six months you're supposed to double your weight, which she did. In a year, you're supposed to triple, which she did. So, there weren't any red flags as far as her weight was concerned. When she hit 10 pounds at six months and started sleeping through the night, she was right on schedule. I mean, I was a very tired mom, but that didn't matter – I walked in her room every hour and half with a smile on my face.

Evan: We both did. We consciously tried never to let Jennifer see or feel that something was wrong.

A persistent cough

Evan: We began to suspect that something might be wrong about the time that Jennifer was 2. What I remember is coughing. She'd get a cold, and then she'd get better, but it would come back and the cough would persist. We got very concerned, and I remember discussing it with the pediatrician. His initial thought was that it was allergies – a good explanation. But, in retrospect, that was the first red flag. We sensed that something was not right.

Donna: So, they tested for allergies, and she was allergic to a lot of things. So, they started giving medicine that would dry her up, which it turns out is the worst thing you can do for a CF child. The mucus is cement-like to begin with and, if you dry things up even more, you could kill the kid. Jennifer ended up in the hospital because of that, and they put her under a mist tent. I slept right beside her.

Evan: And that – a mist tent – also happens to be one of the worst things you can do for CF, but they didn't know that at the time. A mist tent was basically an oxygen tent that they pumped warm, moist air into. But think about it – what does bacteria love? Warm, moist air. Couple that with the CF body's inability to get out the gunk – they can't because the consistency of the mucus in someone with CF is like bubblegum. So, her lungs become a breeding ground for bacteria, and the whole thing creates a vicious circle of infection. They didn't know any better back then.

A characteristic essence

Evan: When Jennifer was a baby and we changed her diaper, that's when we figured something wasn't right. Unfortunately, her digestive system wasn't working properly, and changing her diaper was a monumental task, to say the least. What did we do? We didn't make fun of her. We didn't say, "What's this? Oh, my god!" Instead, we'd make a joke of it. I would say, Woo-ooh, smells like roses! And she'd laugh. Little thing lying on the table just laughing her eyes out.

After I cleaned her up, I put on too much lotion and too much powder, but she smelled so good. I would like to inhale her. I would hold her so tight.

As she got older and became more independent, I would every once in a while grab her and hold her for 5 to 10 seconds, no more. Just enough so I could smell her. It was almost like a narcotic to me.

2 – FEARS ARE CONFIRMED

Jennifer: But the bright future was slowly presenting a huge black dot on the horizon. At the age of 2, I was diagnosed with cystic fibrosis (CF), a genetic killer of a disease, which is slow and merciless in its quest to consume and kill me.

The world turned upside down

Evan: The way it happened in my memory ... the doctor at Skokie Valley came to us and said, "I would like to perform what we call a "sweat test" – I'm sure it's nothing but, to do the right thing, I want to check this out." We said, "Of course."

It turns out the sweat test was developed by a guy named Gibson who happened to be one of Jennifer's original doctors, and they explained how it's done – they'd put gauze on Jennifer's wrist or arm and then attach a metal band that's attached to electricity, and they'd heat the band up. The purpose is to gather sweat, then they analyze it to see what was in there, or what's not in there.

They look for chloride, or salt, because CF patients have a higher degree of salt in their sweat. The problem is that it dries out a person's mucus. For the rest of us, who don't have CF, mucus is an important cleansing agent – it gets the body's gook out wherever it happens to be. Well, with Jennifer and people like her, they can't get out the dried up mucus without a tremendous amount of hard work. You need literally to make yourself cough, which we helped her do in the early days.

After they did the test, we went home, and the doctor called us a day or two later and said, "It came back positive."

Donna: But "don't worry" he said. "Let's make sure. The test could be false."

Evan: He said, "We don't do this test too often, so I recommend that you go down to Children's." He was referring to what in those days was called Children's Memorial Hospital in Lincoln Park, so we took her there.

Again, our heads are in the clouds somewhere, I guess – Jennifer was feeling well, she responded to whatever the hell they did to her, and she was still just Jennifer at age 2½. They did the test, and they said come back the next day, or the day after, something like that. We went back there on October 22nd, 1974 – it was a beautiful day ... no clouds in the sky. We went down there smiling, having fun, and my sister came along with us.

We went in, and the nurse said to my sister, "Why don't take Jennifer and go play?" Okay, not a problem. Meanwhile, Donna and I are sitting in the room and the door opens up, and this man walks in, a doctor. He's all crunched up from cerebral palsy. A typical gait of a cerebral palsy patient, the slur of the voice, and he says, "My name is Dr. Francis Duda." He looked at us and, with a tear in his eye, he said, "I'm so sorry. Jennifer has Cystic Fibrosis."

On hearing the fateful news

Evan: It was the worst day of my life. Even worse than when I lost my dad, and we were never the same after, ever. He talked more and explained certain things, but I don't remember too much of what he talked about.

Donna: My world fell apart. We were in a little room when they told us, and the room got even smaller. I don't even know if I heard all the words. I just know that they told me my daughter had a disease and that it's not good.

Evan: We were with Dr. Duda 45 minutes or so, maybe an hour at most. Then I remember we didn't go home right away. They directed us to what I would call in to-day's terms a department of social services. If I remember correctly they, talked about how to deal with the practical side a little bit. They talked about the cost of dealing with something like this and at that time what state programs may be available. The woman I remember, and I said to myself at the time, "She's just look-ing, reading it off a menu like, almost detached emo-tionally." That's what I remember, and then we went home.

Donna: We didn't really know what Cystic Fibrosis was, but we learned very quickly.

Evan: If I remember correctly, after the initial sweat test at the Skokie Valley, like every other parent we had Dr. Spock's book, so I looked up Cystic Fibrosis, and it scared the hell out of me. I learned enough to know this is bad, this is not good. But, generally, I don't like to worry when there's nothing to worry about – don't put the cart in front of the horse, that kind of thing. After the session at Children's, that all changed, and we suddenly had lots to worry about. Donna and I, I don't know how we did it.

Emotionally, I was very sad. Not only was I sad, but I was also angry. That's what I remember, but I did not show my sadness or anger in front of Jennifer. Jennifer only saw smiles. She was 2½, what the hell does she know? She didn't need to see me cry – that would be unacceptable – and I think that maybe tells you the way Donna and I behaved – not only then but through the whole journey, how we did it.

There is a movie that I love called 'All that Jazz' and it's a story about Bob Fosse, who was a choreographer and a Broadway producer. He was also a messed-up guy. Drugs, alcohol, just messed up, but extremely talented. There's a scene in the movie where he's coming off a binge and he's got to get ready to start a show, and they show him in the shower just standing there letting the water beat on him. Trying to get back to normal, he gets out of the shower and the bathroom is all steamy. So, he takes his towel and he cleans the steam off the mirror, and he looks in the mirror and he goes, "Show time!"

I used that all my career in sales. You walk into a situation, and the potential client could care less that you just had a fight with your husband or your wife. So, it becomes "Show time!" and I used that with Jennifer. She didn't need to know in those early days, and even through most of her life, how hurt I was.

Donna: Even so, I knew she knew. She knew something the day she was diagnosed. She knew something was wrong, and so she did things to entertain us, to make us feel better.

Accepting reality

Evan: Once we accepted the reality, like Donna said, we made a conscious decision – "Okay, let's deal with it." We had a new normal. We didn't spend any time that I can remember, saying, "Oh man!" or "Why me?"

Donna: Never.

Evan: We never said, "why did we end up with the short stick?" We said, "Okay, here is the situation. To the best of our ability let's deal with it," And that's what we did.

Donna: We just started a new normal, and it was medicines and the vitamins, and eating, making sure she's eating properly.

Evan: Getting her rest.

Donna: Getting her rest.

Evan: Being careful with other people.

Donna: Being sure that no one who was sick came into our house, and keeping her as healthy as possible so that when something came along, hopefully a cure, she'd be a candidate for it.

Doing the right thing

Evan: Many people would give into the fear, the frustration, the inability to help. We never did that, ever. There was never, ever a thought, feeling, premonition that we wouldn't do what we had to do. Why? We didn't know how to do it. It wasn't in our DNA.

I believe, and I learned this on my journey, that being negative and giving in and taking the easy way out takes the least amount of energy. Doing the right thing and believing the right thing, whatever the hell that means, that's where the energy goes to.

It's easy to curl up, like when I got sick, and lay in the bed and say, "That's it. I'm out of here." That would have been simple compared to what I've lived through the last four and a half years. I'm not saying I'm better or worse than anyone, but that's who I am, and that's who she was. That's who Jennifer was. She learned it from us. And that's all we know. We're not super human. We just did what we thought was the right thing to do.

It would have been so disrespectful to Jennifer for us to think otherwise, to allow negative thoughts to come into our head.

What is Cystic Fibrosis?

Cystic Fibrosis (CF) is a progressive, genetic disease that causes persistent lung infections and limits the ability to breathe over time. In those with CF, a defective gene (called CFTR) causes mucus and other secretions that are usually thin to become thick & sticky. This thickening of fluids clogs the body's passageways and leads to a host of problems. In the lungs, the mucus clogs airways and traps bacteria, leading to infections, extensive lung damage, and respiratory failure. In the pancreas, the mucus prevents release of digestive enzymes that allow the body to break down food and absorb vital nutrients.

An Inherited Condition, CF is carried by 1 in every 25 people, and the mutated gene must be present from both parents in order for a child to contract the disease. 1 out of every 3,000 newborns is afflicted by CF.

Signs & Symptoms of CF include salty-tasting skin, slow growth and poor weight gain, accumulation of thick sticky mucus, frequent chest & sinus infections, coughing, and shortness of breath. Long term, most individuals with CF eventually die from a CF-related cause, and cardio-respiratory complications account for 80% of those deaths. The median survival age of individuals with CF is about 40 years. (At the time that Jennifer was born, the average life expectancy was 15 years.)

Detection & Diagnosis can be difficult in the early years. In many cases, parents first suspect CF because the baby's skin tastes salty. Individuals with CF have elevated levels of sodium and chloride in their sweat, so the most common form of testing is the (no-needle) **Sweat Test**. Genetic testing is also used to identify the condition.

A Cure for CF has not yet been identified, but there is a great deal of ongoing research & development activity. Fortunately, current treatment management practices now allow for much longer, fuller lives for individuals with CF than was possible previously. The cornerstones of effective management that ease symptoms and reduce complications are: 1) proactive treatment of airway infection, 2) adoption of good nutrition habits, and 3) following an active lifestyle.

For More Information, visit Cystic Fibrosis Foundation (cff.org), CF Roundtable (cfroundtable.com).

3 – THE FIGHT BEGINS

Jennifer: I was also born a fighter with a laugh that echoes throughout the heavens above and a positive attitude that does succumb to the dark side now and then.

Developing a game plan

Evan: Okay, we go home and we start learning as much as we can about Cystic Fibrosis. We get involved with the CF Foundation. We do everything to find out what we can because the diagnosis says she might live to 15. In my thinking, there was no way. She was going to live longer, and I was going to do everything I could to make that happen.

Donna: We started connecting with others right away. We connected with people, we connected with the foundation, we read everything possible. I took Jennifer, and we met some people that had CF children, and we had lunch. Jennifer was about 3 at the time. We found out everything imaginable on what CF was about. We had to know everything because, when they told me that she would live to 15, I wasn't taking that. My daughter would live way past that, and I would do everything in my power to keep her as healthy as possible so that, if and when there was a cure or whatever, she'd be a candidate for it.

Moving into action mode

Donna: We started doing everything they told us to do.
Postural drainage, eating ... I always had her eat the
rights foods, and we decided to give her vitamins since
she was deficient in so many things, and so the journey
began. Jennifer was compliant ... is that the word compliant?

Evan: Oh. yeah, she followed the routine.

Donna: I mean there were no fights, no nothing. It was
what she was supposed to do.

Evan: We tried to make it normal. You have brown hair,
you have CF. That's how we handled it.

Finding a new normal

Evan: After the diagnosis, it took maybe a month to get
to a new normal. It was relatively short and, from the
beginning, we were pretty much always on the same
page. With all of our craziness, Donna and I were on
the same page in terms of Jennifer 99% of the time.
Sometimes not even knowing we were on the same
page. We just were.

What normal looks like

Evan: How can you go from raising a normal, little, 2-
year old child to all of a sudden you're daily routine is
turned upside down? How can that be normal? How
can that not create all kinds of turmoil or conflict, or
whatever?

Donna: Because we made it normal.

Evan: That's what we did. We made it normal. With Jennifer, it was like raising a normal 2-year-old except there was another layer, and we handled that layer in such a way that she just accepted that this was her life. And it's okay. We tried not to make a big deal about anything related to CF.

There was no alternative

Evan: We worked hard to create a warm home environment. We had to – there was no alternative. We could've given in, but we made the conscious decision never to give in. Whether it was in care of Jennifer or in lifestyle, giving up was never an alternative. Just like they said in Apollo 13, "Failure is not an option."

4 – EXTENDED FAMILY NOT ALWAYS A "VILLAGE"

Jennifer: I have wonderful support from my family but, in the end, it is up to me! It is up to me to do all my treatments and do all I can to stay or get healthy.

Dynamics on the maternal side

Evan: Let's start with Donna's father. He really enjoyed Jennifer. You could just feel it. His granddaughter. He already had two from Donna's sister. He just enveloped her immediately, and you could see how happy he was. When the diagnosis came, it affected him big time. Like men of his era, he didn't show much emotion on the outside, but I know he was crying on the inside.

We lived in Evanston then, and Donna's parents lived in Skokie – maybe a 15-minute ride, no more. We would go there a lot in the early days. Donna's mother didn't drive, so we took Jennifer to them. Donna and I, we'd drop Jennifer off, then go to a show. That was never a problem – even after the diagnosis. We didn't let them do the posture drainage but, as far as taking care of Jennifer, that was never an issue.

Donna's mother, she was different. Her background ... her mother died when she was 2½ and her father was left with 6 children. Aunts and uncles took some

of the children. Her mom was placed in an orphanage
for about a year. When her father remarried, he took
her back home. She didn't get along with her step-
mom. I think she may have moved in with her older
sister at some point, although her older sister died
while giving birth. So, Donna's mom didn't have a
great childhood.

Now, Donna's sister, Marilyn - in the early years, she
was very caring, very concerned, very engaged in
Jennifer's care. Like everything, nothing stays the same.
But, in those early years, I give her all the credit in the
world. In the early years, we went on vacation, a con-
vention, once, twice, three times, I don't remember,
and she took care of Jennifer. We couldn't have gone
without her. And Donna's sister has two very wonderful children – Barry and Julie, who both were wonderful cousins to Jennifer. They loved Jennifer from the get
go.

Julie played with her like a big sister would. Made up
all kinds of silly games, played Chutes and Ladders,
things like that ... Barry and Julie were real athletic
also, and they all played tennis, played softball, whatever. Those days were good days. Life changes and, as
all 3 of them got older, they went their own ways. But
they all had a big impact on each other – in fact, that's
why Barry's now a pediatrician, because Jennifer moti-
vated him.

And on the paternal side

Donna: Evan's mom – she was something else. She had
her own problems, mental problems, but I never could

understand why she didn't like me because I put out the red carpet for her all the time.

Evan: She didn't like you because she couldn't control you.

Donna: She broke her leg and was in a wheelchair. She stayed with us for a while. We had a stoop in the foyer, and she had to get up and down to use the other rooms. We had a neighbor install a ramp so she was able to maneuver around. We had a couch that pulled out into a bed, and she slept there in the living room and I took care of her.

Evan: As long as she needed you, she was nice to you.

Donna: I remember she lived on Sheridan Road. One time, I was eight months pregnant, she was having an anxiety attack, and it was snowing. We lived about 30 minutes away, and she wanted Michael to bring her a pack of cigarettes.

I went with him. She lived in a studio apartment and was afraid to be alone, and so Mike and I slept over ... I'm almost to full term, and Mike and I slept in a very small couch bed while she was in the other one. I never felt she liked me.

You know what? She probably liked me. She just didn't know how to show me all the time. This made it hard for me, because I had always been so loved. I got into this family and, while some family members were nice, his mother and several others were horrible. Many of them had bad marriages. And we had a good marriage. I think they held that against us.

Then also, I think because my sister-in-law couldn't have children, as we thought, and here I had my own child, maybe my mother-in-law was angry because her daughter couldn't have a child. I don't know.

Evan: You know what? Don't waste your energy on that.

Evan: With regard to my mother, she was a strange woman. She was the youngest of five. Grew up in the depression. She had a domineering mother and a milk toast of a father, and her older siblings did not treat her fairly. It was not good, and she did not have a good life.

My father, when she met him, was a good-looking guy, and he swept her off her feet. From that point, my mother would live somewhat in a fantasy world – that's how she coped. Unfortunately, over the years, the demons kept coming out and, as she got older, they became stronger. When Jennifer was born, she was sort of there, but not really. When Jennifer was diagnosed, she told me, "Don't expect me to be a normal grand-mother."

When I talk to people who have grandchildren, they say that it is one of the coolest things of all time. It really has to be. My mother couldn't see that. She didn't want to see it, and she wouldn't accept it. She wanted nothing to do with it.

Then she once told me, after Jennifer was diagnosed, she said, "Why do you only talk about CF?" This is my mother. Who the hell am I going to talk to? I went to her, my mother, to tell her that I was concerned about something and that I was scared, and she tells me basi

cally, "Get over it." That was my mother, and it hurt.
Throughout Jennifer's life, she was never really there,
ever. Finally, it got to a point where Jennifer said in
essence, "Screw you." And she was right to do so. It
got so bad that my mother put me in a position where I
had to choose between my wife & daughter and her.
Obviously, who did I choose? There was no choice.
Unfortunately, it took me about 20 years before I woke
up to that reality.

Moving, along on my side of the family ... My sister
had three children – two adopted, Jimmy and Scotty,
and Elizabeth, the youngest, was their biological child.
They were pretty close in age to Jennifer, but they were
troubled children and didn't treat Jennifer right. From
an early age all the way through, Scott, who was in the
same class as Jennifer, showed a mean streak. Jimmy,
the oldest one had serious mental problems. He finally
died from alcoholism as an adult.

My sister and my brother-in-law, forgive me, were
not good parents. Not at all, and they paid for it. You
might think it's cute when the kids are little to have no
discipline but, when they're 15 and they tell you to go
screw yourself, you look at them and say, "I gave you
everything. Why are you treating me like that?" Because of what you did when they were 2, that's why.
Duh. People don't understand that. That was my sister.

So, our immediate family was kind of a mixed bag in
terms of what we had to deal with. But, unlike so many
lucky families dealing with Cystic Fibrosis who come
together in strength because of their adversity, we
were not so fortunate. If it takes a village, this was our
village. There was nobody there that we could cry

with, that could hold us and say I feel it, I feel your pain. There was nobody there. And, in light of that, what Donna and I were able to accomplish was remarkable. Two crazy little kids. It's amazing what the hell we did.

Donna's parents were available for some support, and her sister helped a lot, especially in the beginning, but it was not enough. They did the best they could, unlike my mother who is just a bad person.

5 – JENNIFER THRIVES IN YOUTH

Jennifer: I have been active my whole life. I have played tennis, baseball, run, and more. I have also been a swimmer my whole life. I have never been afraid of the water because I always knew what a strong swimmer I was.

Growing up I was strong and taught to be a fighter, confront each battle with CF and keep myself as healthy as possible to win the CF war.

Different homes

Evan: Jennifer's first home was in Evanston. We lived there when Jennifer was born, and we were there a year, maybe two.

Donna: 3 years.

Evan: Then we moved from there to Glenview to another apartment, and we were there until Jennifer was …

Donna: 5½

Evan: 5½. We stayed there in Glenview and then we ended up in Deerfield, and we were there 20 some years. Deerfield is what Jennifer thought of as her childhood home.

Donna: But she remembered Glenview for sure because we made a lot of friends who are still our friends.

Friendly neighborhood

Donna: When we lived in Deerfield, we lived in a town-house and, in that neighborhood, everybody would regularly be outside in nice weather, like having a party ...

Evan: Every night. A lot of young families, and all the kids were out running and playing. In those days, kids had what they used to call "Hot Wheels" – tricycles designed low to the ground – and they would be flying around and, oh my god, we had so much fun!

Donna: Yeah, we had a lot of fun. Evan's cousin lived across the street from us. They had a little girl, and they were always at my house. They'd always eat at my house.

Evan: Because they never had food in their house.

Donna: The mother wasn't real good at that but, anyways, one time our cousin's little girl, Cari, came over and said, "Aunt Donna, what's for dinner?" because she was just used to eating at my house all the time. To make a point, I go, "Go ask your mother." That was a funny thing.

Fun at the pool

Donna: There was a pool where we lived. We had so much fun at the pool.

Evan: Lot of good times with the pool. I taught her how to swim when she was maybe 5. There weren't any swimming-related concerns because of her CF. But there was a kid who pushed her in the pool and I had to save her.

Donna: Yes, she was 3 years old, and she was playing a game with a boy who was about a year older. Jennifer would push him from the side of the pool into the water. He'd get out, she'd push him again, he'd get out, she'd push him again, he'd get out, push him again. Finally, he decided he would push her. So, the boy pushed Jennifer in – it was like 3 feet of water – and Evan flew in in seconds, scraped his leg to get her out because she couldn't swim. The little boy just was devastated because he didn't mean anything. They just had McDonalds, and the boy threw his up. He was so upset because he didn't want to hurt her. He didn't know she couldn't swim.

Fairness

Evan: She always wanted people to be fair. I mean, she understood completely that not everything goes your way, not every decision is in your favor. Just be fair. She was into that, and she liked people that were truthful. Tell me what the deal is and I'll deal with it.

So, truthfulness, fairness, and understanding I think would be a good word, too. Those are values that Jennifer cared about.

Excited about school

Donna: I can remember how she just was so excited about going to school, because she was an extrovert.

She loved people, she loved to have fun, she loved everything.

Evan: She wasn't afraid of the separation ... She didn't have any separation anxiety. We did, which she didn't know about. For her, it was a new adventure, and that's the way I would talk to her, "It's a new adventure. It's going to be so exciting." I'd build it up to make her feel like, "Oh, yeah, let's go."

Off to kindergarten

Donna: We moved to Deerfield when Jennifer was 5½, and she was going to start kindergarten. Well, the day the bus came for her to take her to kindergarten I thought I'd have a heart attack because she was leaving me. I think I can't deal with people leaving me.

We lived on the main street where the bus would pick her up, and we all went to the bus stop that day. It was very difficult but I couldn't keep her from leaving. So, all right, she goes to school. That was everyday – from my patio, I would watch the bus go by and I'd see her little face and she'd be waving. And I waved back Then I couldn't wait till she got home.

It's funny because other parents would tell me, you know when summer comes and they're sending their kids to camp, they couldn't wait to get rid of them, and stuff like that. I never could understand them because I never wanted Jennifer to be away from me.

Telling her teachers about CF

Donna: She started kindergarten, and I had to tell all the teachers because she ate lunch there and she would come with a little container that had chocolate syrup in it. The teachers had to mix her pills in the chocolate syrup and give it to her. The pills were enzymes that had to be taken before each meal to help her digest the food properly.

Evan: Mucus in the pancreas clogs the ducts and makes it so that, whatever the pancreas does, it can't do. The medication in those early days was called Pancreaze. It was needed to help CF kids digest their foods because the pancreas can't do its job.

Donna: That was kindergarten and she was such a happy kid. She loved to have fun, loved to giggle, and afterwards the kids loved to come to my house, because I'd play with them.

Evan: And feed them.

Donna: And feed them. Yeah, I would play with them and feed them, and I probably was the same height as them so they felt very comfortable. I was like one of them.

Getting support from schools

Evan: Even in the early days – first grade, second grade, fourth grade, whatever – we made a conscious effort to stay in contact with Jennifer's teachers, especially if she had to be out of school for any period of time. We wanted to make sure that she kept up with her homework.

They were all wonderful. The teachers and administrators of the schools – they were kind, caring, concerned. They understood. I think some were even amazed at her academic ability given what she was dealing with. She never fell behind, ever.

Donna: The principal wrote a letter to us once.

Evan: Mr. Bassofin.

Donna: He adored her. I remember in his letter he said that he hopes his children are like Jennifer.

Evan: He didn't need to say that ...

Success in school

Evan: In terms of her performance in school, she had good grades, B+ average. She was very concerned about her work and never ever did not turn something in. And we didn't have to tell her, "Sit down and do your homework." After she got home from school, Donna would give her some food, and she'd sit down and do her work. After that, she went out and played. We didn't tell her. That's just what she did.

Donna: She did. She came home from school, and did her homework. I've had people say to me, "Oh, my god, my daughter, my son won't do their homework," and I can't relate to that.

Evan: It just carried over. My dad used to tell me, and I told her, "If you've got something to do, do it." She was much better at it than I ever was, much better. Like I said earlier, she was listening.

A superior athlete ... selectively

Evan: The effects of CF, what I call the unrelenting savagery, begins to take over as the person gets older. But, one of the unique things about CF is that, in the early days, you can't tell. A CF person looks absolutely normal, and CF kids for the most part can be active just like other kids.

Donna: Jennifer was active physically, but some sports were hard for her because of all the running up and down. Also, she was always little compared to her peers. But she did basketball in grammar school in fifth, sixth grade. And, in high school, she took tennis up. She played singles. I remember watching one match – she got stung by a bee, and she just kept going.

Evan: She became a great swimmer to the best of her ability. We also got her involved with softball in Deerfield. Deerfield in those days had a great girls softball league, and it was a really big deal. She played for, I don't know, from about age 7 to maybe 14 – she was in the eighth grade.

Donna: She was the pitcher.

Evan: I wanted to keep everything normal, but I also knew I had to control the CF without her knowing that I was controlling it. I was the team manager every year. I was the boss. Did I want to do that? Not really, but I did it. My ulterior motive was that I could watch her, and I could protect her. I couldn't give it off to some other man to take care of her. I took care of her.

Never a homerun

Evan: Jennifer was a very good athlete. Donna and I both had good hand-eye coordination, and Jennifer got that, which is a cornerstone to being a good athlete. She understood it, and she could do it. Physically, she definitely had some issues – like she could never run, but neither could I. We used to laugh when she played softball. She made the all-star team every year, on traveling teams, and was a great pitcher, but she couldn't run like the other girls. Not because she was out of breath, she just couldn't run, like me. We tried to make light of it, but in all those years she played softball, she never hit a home run. Came close a couple of times, but never was able to circle the bases. She could just never get around in time.

THE NEWSLETTER OF THE CYSTIC FIBROSIS FOUNDATION   NORTHERN ILLINOIS CHAPTER

6 N. MICHIGAN AVENUE. CHICAGO, IL 60602 (312) 236-4491   OCTOBER 1982

Jennifer Codell Named To Little League All-Stars

Jennifer Codell, 10, daughter of Mike Codell, prominent member of our Board of Directors, made baseball headlines in Little League circles this year.

An outstanding pitcher for the ROBBINS in the Deerfield Little League, she posted a 13-1 won-lost record during the regular season, and went 5-0 in the playoffs, to lead her team to the division championship. Jennifer also posted a .786 batting average.

As a result of her outstanding performance, she was named a divisional All-Star and was one of only 10 players, out of 85, chosen for the traveling All-Star team.

6 – ALL IS NOT AS IT APPEARS ...

Jennifer: *Unfortunately, when dealing with a chronic illness, bad things happen, and you have to prepare for the worse-case scenario but then to stay optimistic and fight all the way through – to keep adjusting the sails but to be aware that a storm can come in and blow me off course. Then I adjust the sails again and again.*

Father sees red

Evan: It's important to know that I was a fighter when I was a kid. Oh, yeah, I always fought. I was always either the littlest or the one with biggest head of white curly hair on the playground. You talk about bullying today, it was around back then, too. I realized I would never be the biggest kid on the block, but I could be among the strongest and meanest and that's what I became. After a couple incidents when I was maybe 10 to 12, it never happened again. There were two suspensions that I served from Evanston Township High School and New Trier High School because of fighting and almost killing the gym teacher by forcing his head in a locker.

I had some anger management problems back in the day, but that was my father, too. He had to come and pick me up and he said, "What happened?" I told him. He looked at me and he said, "Good. Let's go home."

My dad grew up in LA, and he went to Hollywood High School, where antisemitism was rampant – not just there, but everywhere. His last name was Cohen, and he had to fight his way home every day. He did, and that's what he taught me. He said, "You might go down, but you can't walk away." That transferred over, not only in dealing with Jennifer and dealing with Donna's sickness, both of which were tough. But it was not a good approach long-term. Once you reach adulthood, you can't go smack someone in the face. That wasn't right.

Anyway, after we got Jennifer's diagnosis and things built up in me, sometimes I'd be driving somewhere, and I'd start screaming, using profanity, anger, terrible anger, but never in the house. Absolutely not. You can't do that, that would be ridiculous. I didn't take out my frustrations on Jennifer let alone on Donna. So, instead, I screamed and yelled, and went to the gym and got incredibly big and strong. That's where my energy was. That's how I let off the steam but, in the house, and in our little family, never ... other than the one night with the pizza when Donna and I were having an argument like any married couple has, totally stupid and ridiculous, I don't remember what it was about. Probably my mother. We decided to order a pizza from Lou Malnati's – at that time we lived in Evanston, and the closest one was in Lincoln Wood, so I went and got it. Came back, and I'm still angry from the argument. I open up the pizza, and it's the wrong pizza. So, I kind of roared in anger and frustration and threw the pizza against the wall. After a little while, I scraped the pizza off the wall, put in the box, took it back, and said, "You gave me the wrong damn pizza." I came home with the right pizza.

So, anger management - that's how I handled it but, unfortunately for Donna, her demons came out. The agoraphobia and the panic attacks ... It was terrible.

Mother feels safety ... at home

Donna: What happened to me is I became anxiety stricken after Jennifer was diagnosed. I developed agoraphobia – it's being afraid of the "marketplace," but for me I felt unsafe anywhere outside the home. There was a time there I couldn't even go to my mailbox. I was afraid of everything. I couldn't drive by myself. With friends, I managed to get Jennifer to wherever she had to go. I managed to do my shopping. One of my friends didn't have a car and I had a car and, as long as someone was with me, I was okay driving. Even though I had all these problems, I always managed to deal with the problem and in a good way.

Evan: Jennifer's condition was the trigger. I mean I'm no psychiatrist – what the heck do I know? – but I would say the shock of Cystic Fibrosis triggered what more than likely was already in Donna. It was such a devastating realization that it like exploded out of her and manifested itself as agoraphobia. I give Donna all the credit in the world because she did survive, and she did not show any of this to Jennifer in the early days and when Jennifer was little. Donna never wanted Jennifer to feel guilty that somehow she hurt her mother. Donna deserves a huge amount of credit for that.

Donna: Jennifer didn't know anything about it when she was little. When she got older, I'm sure she knew. Jennifer didn't have a sibling. I was not only her mother, but I was also her sister and we would do things like sisters would do. We were very, very close.

Today, I am better. 100% better. I would say my worst time was when Jennifer was 3½ to age 16, 18, sometime around then. I think it was when Jennifer went away to college that I started to get a little bit better ...

Evan: I think it was more gradual. As Donna learned more about what was going on inside of her, it answered questions I guess, so it enabled her to deal with it. Over the years, it got better. Some of it was by necessity, and some of it was just because it was. That's what I think. But it was tough – it was tough on Donna, and it was tough on me.

Donna: Here's a for instance – we went to the show, the movie theatre, I can remember it was in Highland Park, and I could feel that it was coming, the panic attack, and I'm thinking, "Oh shoot. oh God, I don't want to tell him, because I knew he would get mad. What am I going to do?" Finally, I couldn't handle it anymore, and I said, "We got to go home." I can remember starting to walk out of the theater, and he took the door and he just slammed it open, and everyone else is still trying to watch the show. I just cringed.

Evan: I know my behavior was unacceptable.

Donna: I would cringe, but I would try to keep it from him ... as much as I could until I couldn't anymore.

And some people said bad things to me. I mean, like, his mother said to me, "You know he might divorce you." I just love her.

Donna's fix-it gene

Donna: I was the youngest of the whole family and, as a result, cousins and everybody doted on me. "Little Donna" they called me, and I was little all the time. I was one of the littlest persons in my class, so I came to be known with my mouth – I was very loud. It also made me very competitive, and I aspired to be the best I could be in sports, but in other areas, too.

I came from a very loving family. They just loved me to pieces, and the whole family just exuded love. All of that made me a caring, loving person. My father once made the observation, "Donna, if you were in a room and there was someone in a wheelchair and someone playing basketball, you would go to the person in the wheelchair first." And he's right, I would. I always want to help people, I don't know why but I just want to make things better for other people.

Evan: I know why, because Donna has a gene that is weird, and I call it the fix-it gene. Donna needs to fix everything and, when she can't, it creates a huge level of frustration, and I can't emphasize that enough. Dealing with Jennifer and realizing that she couldn't fix it, and then having to deal with me, it all has driven her nearly insane.

A sense of dizziness

Donna: I began to have dizzy spells. I got dizzy when I was looking up. Even now, if I look up, you can see my eyes do funny things. Playing tennis I have to do things a little different. Like when the ball goes over my head. Around this time, I read a book about vertigo and that, if you have vertigo, that can cause panic attacks. So, I'm going, "Terrific, that's the problem. I'm going to find out ..."

Evan: "... I'm not mentally ill."

Donna: "... I'm not crazy." Turns out I have some benign tumors on my brain. I was probably born with them, and they said, "You take medication for the dizziness, and you'll be fine."

But that's how it started with me going to the doctors and finding out that I had the agoraphobia. It wasn't the tumors – the medicine they gave me wasn't the answer for the panic attacks.

Actually, when they told me that I had tumors, I was already digging my grave. I thought, "That's it, I'm dead." I got even more panicky.

I learned to live with it, but what happened is Jennifer's diagnosis. I saw the diagnosis, became afraid of everything, and I then I had to deal with it.

Stress levels rise

Donna: I became slowly afraid of everything, but I never showed Jennifer.

Evan: Jennifer never saw, but it put tremendous stress on our marriage. Let alone dealing with Cystic Fibrosis and dealing with Jennifer, just the dealings between a husband and wife ...

Donna: And your mother.

Evan: It was terrible.

Donna: It wouldn't happen at home. My safety was to be home. It was when I had to go out ...

For example, I play tennis, that was my outlet, to hit the ball as hard as I could and pretend the ball was Cystic Fibrosis. But one time I was out of tennis balls, so I put Jennifer in the car, went to the store to get some tennis balls. I'm in line, and the panic attack hits so hard I can't stay. So, I put the tennis balls back, grab Jennifer, put her in the car, and go home.

After that, I couldn't drive by myself. That's how panic stricken I was, my anxiety. And I worried, how am I going to do things like go grocery shopping? I can't go by myself. Well, there was a friend of mine who didn't have a car, so she and I, and the kids, would go in my little car. We had these two little people in the back seat, and we had to pile groceries on top of them. And that's how I did my stuff. My friends became aware because I had to tell them, and some were more supportive than others.

A consistent challenge

Donna: There was one time ... we were invited to a wedding, it was downtown, and at the last minute it's like,

"I can't go." The cousin who was getting married called me up afterwards and said how selfish I was that I couldn't come. I mean, she just reamed me unbelievable. It was especially difficult because I wasn't doing something because I wanted to, I was doing something because I was just panic stricken, and his family was horrible to me.

Evan: It was bad because not only was I dealing with Jennifer, but I also had to deal with Donna's situation. And everything was not peaches and cream – there were many dark times. I've never had the urge – like some people I have heard about with chronically ill children – to run away, to abandon Jennifer and Donna. But I was in as much pain as Donna was – it just manifested differently.

Donna: There were times when we had to go to Children's, and the panic would come as we got closer. My aunt happened to live on the way, so I'd say, "I can't go – you have to drop me off at Aunt Shirley's." He would drop me off and go by himself. Or other times we'd be at the hospital and you had to take me to my aunt's, because I couldn't stay. It just was difficult for Evan, but ...

Evan: We got through it.

Donna: It was a difficult time. Nobody understood panic attacks, and I was embarrassed to tell people that I had this condition unless I really had to. It was difficult.

Evan: I have to say that difficult is not a strong enough word. It was way beyond difficult ...

Social life diminished

Evan: To expand on Donna's situation from my perspective, I already mentioned the amount of stress that it put on our relationship as a husband and a wife, but it also severely impacted our social life. I mean we were still young vibrant people, wanting to go and see and do, and I had a very hard time for many years accepting it, to be honest.

Like most mental illness, it's mostly misunderstood, especially by people who have never experienced mental illness or who are not educated in mental illness. "What do you mean you can't drive to the store? What do you mean you can't go to the wedding? What do you mean you can't go visit? What are you? What are you talking about?"

Finding ways

Donna: I found ways to do the things I had to do. Jennifer, she took tennis lessons, ice-skating lessons, dance. I just found a way to be able to get her where she needed to go.

Evan: Donna was unbelievable in the way she could manipulate the situation and the people in order to accomplish what she needed to get done. "Manipulate" is sometimes an ugly word, but I really just mean that she was resourceful.

Donna's struggle never really stopped. The struggle was always there. The fear was always there. All that stuff never went away, but we learned to deal with it.

Complementing each other

Evan: One thing I've noticed as I look back on those
days is that Donna and I made a pretty good tag team.
When Jennifer was feeling good, okay, I was fine, and
Donna was a mess. But, on the reverse side, when
Jennifer got sick, I went bonkers, and Donna took over.
We didn't discuss it. We didn't plan it. It just hap-
pened.

But if we had been out of sync and we were both
bonkers at the same time, who would have paid the
price? Jennifer. She needed at least one of us, and that's
what we gave her.

It took us both to survive

Evan: Right in the beginning is when it started. When
Jennifer was feeling good, meaning when we weren't
dealing with any issues with her other than normal issues, I was fine, not a problem. But Donna was a mess.
The agoraphobia, or what other issues she may have
been dealing with, but to give Donna credit, we recognized it – it wasn't controlling our lives – but she was a
mess.

On the other hand, as soon as Jennifer got sick,
whether it was just at home, or unfortunately if we had
to go to the hospital, I became the mess, and Donna became the strong one. I have no idea why. It's just a
good thing we had each other. We played off of each
other, we used each other, gave each other strength
when we individually were at our weakest points.

Doing what felt right

Evan: More times than not, not knowing what we were doing, we did what felt right. We disagreed on occasion, of course. Fought on occasion, yes. But most times, we never lost the focus on Jennifer – what's best for her, not what's best for us. For whatever reason, our strengths melded. We took strengths from both of us for each other, and I do believe that Jennifer took a lot of our strengths, as any child would, and our negatives, too. You know, let's be honest. As I said before, she never walked on water. But that's what made her.

Having other children

Donna: I wanted four children. When Jennifer was diagnosed at age 2½, that's about the time we would otherwise have been thinking about having another child. But, after the CF diagnosis, I was trying to keep Jennifer alive and keep me out of a mental institution. There was no way I was having another child because of that and, second, I would not bring another child into the world with such a high chance of having CF.

Evan: Donna's absolutely right, and there's also a third reason that made us decide not to have additional children. When you have multiple children, when one gets sick, they all get sick. Then the parents get sick. We couldn't afford to expose Jennifer to that.

Donna: It wouldn't be fair to Jennifer, it wouldn't be fair to the other child, and it wouldn't be fair to all of us. It just wasn't in the cards. I always taught Jennifer that life is like a poker hand – you get the hand, and you play it the best you can. That's what we did.

Evan: Donna and I sat down as adults, as much as we could be adults in those days, and made a decision – that's it, we're done. Now, you could talk to multiple parents with kids who have CF and they have lots of other kids – it worked for them. I can't compare myself to anyone else. We made the decision for ourselves.

Donna: I asked my father, who was a gambler type of person, and he said, "Go ahead. Gamble, go for it."

Evan: We felt you can't play with someone's life. How would you answer this question? "Hey, Dad, did you know that I may get Cystic Fibrosis?" How the hell do you answer that question?

Donna: With Jennifer, I worried that she might say someday, "You gave me Cystic Fibrosis." She never once said that. But, if I brought another child into the world, that might happen, where the child says, "You knew I could have that, why did you do that?" How do you answer? Of course, nowadays you can tell ahead of time with an amniocentesis. But then the question is – you find out, now what do you do? Abort the child?

Evan: Now you're dealing with all kinds of issues. Forget about Cystic Fibrosis. Now you're dealing with the pro-choice, pro-life, whatever. We didn't need all that. Our energy was so concentrated on this little baby that we either consciously, but probably more unconsciously, decided between us that all of our energy need to go right to that.

An only child

Donna: Having an only child can be tricky – I feel that a high percentage of only children are very selfish, and it is all about them. I didn't want that to be for Jennifer. I wanted her to be able to get along with everyone, and not be selfish and do the best that she could do. It was a challenge, because it's very easy to give in to a sick child, because you don't want them to hurt. You feel bad. But I had to make her the best person that she could be – for herself and with other people too.

I'm the type of person that likes to help people, and I really like everyone to like me. I try and do the best I can with everybody.

I think I'm a lot like my father. He was a very strong person, very giving person. I don't know, I just ... I guess I followed in his footsteps. And I came from such a loving family – everybody loved me so much that I was able to ... love others.

Like a sister

Donna: She really did have a sister. She had me. For example, he came home one day and Jennifer and I were arguing, and he started reprimanding both of us. I go, "Wait a minute, I'm the mother. I'm not the child." But that's the way it was ... you know, I was her mother. I was her friend. I was her sister. We were everything to each other.

Tight bond

Donna: She and I had a bond that was unbelievable. One story, when she was studying, doing her homework ... I never had to tell her do your homework or anything.

She'd come home from school, she'd do her homework, and that was it. Very good student. Anyway, she was doing her homework, then she got slap happy and we got laughing hysterically. Then we heard him come in, and she goes, "Oh, the papa's home." And I went, "Oh, the papa. Oh, the papa," and we start clapping our hands. And all of a sudden, we started doing this routine – "Oh, the papa" – and I taped it. It was amazing what was coming out of our mouths. I have the tape. It's hysterical. Jennifer finally said, "Mom, I got to study."

7 – MANAGING MEDICAL CHALLENGES

Jennifer: CF is a part of me just like my brown eyes and my brown hair, so I feel, of course, it is going to influence how I deal with all situations in my life. Dealing with a chronic illness makes one grow up real fast because one is faced with challenges and decisions beyond her years.

Medical advances

Evan: Regarding medical advances with CF, we found that the medical community moved like snails when it came to giving up treatment methods that didn't seem to be working – like the mist tents. It's very hard for those people to accept they may be wrong in their established practices. They'll actually even fight new approaches, to the detriment of patients and the community at-large. Donna and I never accepted the doctors' word as sacred – we respected them as doctors but they surely did not walk on water.

One thing that Donna and I have proven over the years is that we are street smart. If something doesn't feel right, if it doesn't smell right, if it doesn't look right, we'd say, "Wait a minute. This feels wrong."

Following the doctor's orders?

Donna: One of the things that the doctors advised early on that we didn't feel was right was to let her rest, to have her live a largely sedentary lifestyle. And we said, no way. Jennifer was going to be athletic, she was going to do sports, we were going to have fun, and she was going to get the body moving so that the lungs ... so that the lungs would get strong. We didn't listen to them about that.

Evan: Not at all, we totally ... and maybe this is too strong of a word ... but we totally dismissed that. It's unacceptable, one of my favorite words. "I'm sorry pal, it's unacceptable. She's going to be moving." Like I said about the mist tent, what are you nuts? To lay there and to breath in that garbage? "Get off your ass and let's go" – and that's the way I used to talk to her. "Let's go, come on, come on, let's go."

There were many things they told us that we did follow, absolutely. Like the importance of postural drainage and the medications. But there were no checklists – I would say that 80-90% of how Jenifer was raised in the early days was based on what we thought was the right thing to do.

Have fun

Evan: In the simplest terms, we always tried to make things fun. That's the way we lived our life. We try to make it fun. You don't have to spend a huge amount of dollars to have fun, which is a good thing because we didn't have a huge amount of dollars. But dollars and fun, they don't always equate. Fun usually comes from people who enjoy being with each other and doing things together.

The Postural Drainage family game

Donna: Our whole life changed. We had to do postural drainage, which is done with a cupping of the hand, and you thump in the chest area in the front and then in the back. She laid across us ...

Evan: Her head was lower than her feet, and the whole purpose of it was to loosen the mucus and create coughing which would allow her to get the junk out. We had to do this multiple times a day, sometimes as many as six. If she was sick and congested, we'd do it around the clock.

It was devastating at first but, like water seeking its own level, life became normal for two young parents whose only child has Cystic Fibrosis. That was our world, and we were normal in our world.

Donna: We made sure she did everything a child would do growing up. Other than having Cystic Fibrosis, and having to take medicine, and having to do postural drainage, we kept it as normal as possible.

Evan: Even doing the postural drainage we turned it into a game. We would sit on the couch more times than not, and TV would be on, and I'd put a pillow on our laps and Jennifer would lay down with her head on an angle. And we would pound away. I would say 15 to 20 minutes, sometimes longer, sometimes less.

Donna: I made it a game. I pretended she was a drum, and as I was drumming, I would sing a song.

Evan: We would laugh and sing, we would watch TV, we talked, and eventually as Jennifer got older, she'd say, "What's going on? Come on Dad, I got to get going here."

We didn't call it postural drainage, we called it The Exercise. "It's time for The Exercise," and we never missed doing it. When I say never, I mean never. Our

attitude was always, and I told Jennifer this an un-
godly amount of times, "You have to be strong so
when the cure comes you'll be ready."

Donna: I can remember being out late and doing the
postural drainage in the car so that when we got home
she could go right to sleep. It had to be done. There
was no way we were missing it.

In terms of frequency, if Jennifer was okay, we'd have
to do it in the morning and before bed.

Evan: But, if she got a cold or got congested, then it was
up to us to determine how many times we would do it.
In doing that, we'd try to maintain a balance in Jennifer
– physically and emotionally. Physically, because re-
peated tapping hurts, over and above the pain from
coughing for a period of time. Emotionally, we didn't
want Jennifer to think that it was a big deal.

Basically, we were two scared parents trying to do
everything to keep her healthy within a normal routine. All that hard work that Donna and I put into the
early years created the foundation of care that Jennifer
embraced.

As she grew older and she slowly began taking over
her own care, I used to tell her that it's like brushing
your teeth in the morning. Do you think about it or do
you just do it? You just do it – same thing with this,
you just do it. That was mainly my attitude. And she
never resisted. Now, we tried to have a good time with
it.

One aspect of this has to do with the expulsion of gas.
Like all little kids, Jennifer she was fascinated and was

highly entertained by the expulsion of gas, especially her own. Well, with CF kids, unfortunately their digestive tracks are all messed up, which results in terrible stools and terrible gas. At some point, Jennifer realized that passing gas caused a significant reaction from both of us, and so she would do it regularly and on purpose while we were in the middle of postural drainage. Jennifer would laugh, Donna would gag and turn blue, and I who wouldn't give into her would say. "Jennifer, it smells like roses."

Fighting spirit

Donna: We were fighters. We were fighters till the end, and we were very competitive, all of us. If you take fighting and competitiveness together, it's very strong.

Donna: One of the big pieces of advice to Jennifer – that we drilled into her – was to never give up.

Evan: That's a good one.

Donna: Never give up ... It makes me think of a necklace that I bought for Jennifer that said, "Never give up." I sent it to her, but she never got the necklace. It got there when I was there for her funeral, so I gave it to her best friend.

Never give up. Never give up hope. Never give up fighting. Never give up ...

Evan: ... on anything.

Donna: Never give up on anything.

You get 24 hours

Evan: Jennifer had fun. She was a fun person. She wasn't sitting around saying, "Whoa is me."

Donna: Never.

Evan: Even when she was sick, sick. When she was feeling really bad or if something really bad happened, I used to tell her, "You know what? It's okay to be angry. It's okay to be pissed off, frustrated, use whatever word you want. Absolutely normal. Here's the thing. You only get 24 hours. The next day when the sun comes up, you start anew. You cannot ever allow it to carry over to the next day, and she didn't.

What I tried to instill in her was that, after you think something through and you've considered all the angles, and you still determine that the decision is the right one, then you've got to move forward.

Interacting with other children with CF

Evan: It wasn't good for Jennifer to be with other CF children. We didn't know that at first – nobody did. They used to have camps for CF kids that people would donate money to, and they would send their CF kids off to some camp for a week or whatever. But they stopped doing it, and Jennifer never participated.

Donna: I think there was one hospitalization when she had a roommate. But as Jennifer grew older, they realized that it was not good for CF kids to mingle because they could give this certain bacteria to each other that could kill them.

Evan: We all carry this bacteria, called pseudomonas, and to everyone without CF it means nothing from nothing. But, within the CF community, it's not good. It's a huge concern when they're in the hospital, trying to avoid other CF-ers and especially making sure that they didn't room together. Jennifer almost always had a private room.

Jennifer's first hospitalization

Donna: When she was 7, Jennifer ended up at Children's Memorial.

Evan: I was in the ambulance with her. You talk about scared. I don't remember the people. I just remember the lights, and the siren. Terrible. No parent should ever see their kid like that. A little person ... I couldn't do anything.

Donna: We thought we were losing her then.

Evan: Yeah, we thought she was gone.

Donna: She had pneumonia. She had pleurisy. She was very sick, and she even was hallucinating. She was a very, very sick little girl, and that was the time we stayed at Children's. We couldn't stay in the room but they had a bed a for us in the hallway, where Evan and I slept, if you want to call it sleeping. But she bounced back ...

Evan: More times than we can count.

Evan: Jennifer's pattern was pretty consistent. If Jennifer became over-tired, she would get sick. That's just

Jennifer. We were very careful to make sure that she got as much rest as possible and, in this one case, it was just another occurrence of getting sick, getting a cold. But, unlike other times it didn't get better, it got worse. We kept dealing with it as it got worse. Finally, the doctor said she had to go to Children's, so she was taken there in an ambulance.

Jennifer was in the hospital for about 10 days. In the early years, she was hospitalized multiple times – usually once or twice a year – and the general protocol required 10 days in the hospital on average because of the IV treatment. Then she would come home, and it was another 5 to 7 days of recuperation at home. She didn't go right back to school. She got some rest and built up her strength and, only when we felt she was strong enough, she went back to school. But she kept up with her school work. We got all her work and she would do it in the hospital.

New new normal

Evan: We kept getting new normals. You can call it stages, call it whatever you want, but there was no, "Okay, I'm here now, and that's where I'm at." No, that's not the way it was. Nothing stayed the same. Each day, each month, each year was different. We just went with the flow. But the general orientation was to make things "normal" regardless of what it was.

A good example of this was probably one of the hardest things I had to do. In the early days, the normal protocol was 10 to 14 days in the hospital, which was dictated by the antibiotic treatment. Well, as time went on, because of advances in medicine and the pressure to reduce the length of hospital stays, we would get Jennifer to the hospital, and she'd be there, let's say 4, 5 days. Like I said, things change

Then, after we left the hospital, we had to continue the IV treatments at home. The needle was in – the only thing Donna and I had to do was change the bags with the antibiotic and saline solution. We had a schedule, we had an IV pole, we did everything the nurses did. They taught us what to look for and if we saw it call immediately, all that kind of stuff. We were fine with all that, we were good, and Jennifer was good with that, and we were so thankful that she was home because, when Jennifer was in the hospital, I would get up extra-early so that I could have breakfast with her every morning. Then I'd go to work, and we would go back there late afternoon, and we would stay there until, I don't know, 8:00, 9:00, 10:00, whatever. We didn't pay attention to visiting hours, we didn't care. The whole thing was terrible on us. It just almost killed us sometimes.

Well, one time we encountered a new new normal. This one time we met a different protocol – the doctor said we're going to use a new type of antibiotic, but the only way it can be administered is by injection. So, Miss Big Shot – my dear wife –says, "I can do it. Oh, I can do it."

Donna: I practiced on an orange.

Evan: The shot had to be given in Jennifer's thigh, and Miss Big Shot says, "I can do it." But, guess what, she couldn't do it.

Donna: I could not do it, so Mr. Little Shot had to do it.

Evan: As Mighty Mouse once said, "Tah taraah! Here I come to save the day!" But, truthfully, I remember that the level of turmoil inside my body could not be measured. Off the charts. Jennifer never saw it. I'd say, "All right, let's go," and she would lie on Donna's bed, on her side of our bed, and I took her thigh as they taught us, and I squeezed it. I took this syringe, put it in, took it out, and I can't remember if we used a warm cloth or a cold cloth, to put it on afterwards. But it was done, and it was terrible.

Significant medical providers

Evan: On Jennifer's team of medical providers over the years, I can only think of two to be honest who were significant. One was Jerry Kraut. He was her doctor at Children's when he was a resident and, when he got through with that, Lutheran General hired him to start a CF clinic. Jennifer was his first patient, and the first patient at Lutheran General for CF, and of course she was hospitalized. I remember one time we went there for a visit and we walk in her room, and there is Dr. Kraut sitting on her bed playing a board game with her.

Donna: He had no patients but her.

Evan: Then there was a nurse there whose name, if I'm not mistaken, was Irene. Big woman, I mean big. Not just tall, but a big woman, and a wonderful woman.

Donna: Margaret.

Evan: Margaret, that's right. Thank you. I can remember that she was kind, truthful. Jennifer seemed to like her. And there were others who were kind, too. Like the head IV lady – the one they called when they were having trouble getting the IV in. She was very nice. And there was a young woman – a social worker type of person – who played with the kids. She was nice, too. Kindness. I guess that's what I looked for. That's all we ever wanted. Just be kind.

In general, there is no question in my mind that Jennifer received the best possible care available.

Donna: The best.

Evan: No second guessing. I mean, Children's Memorial Hospital, where the hell are you going to go that's better? If we'd had lived in the middle of Nebraska, that would be a different issue, but we live in Chicago, so that wasn't an issue at all.

Creative solutions are sometimes required

Evan: Jennifer was in the hospital a lot for what they used to call, and they still do, tune-ups. When the bacteria reaches a certain point, they need to get it back under control again with IV treatments, which can be very traumatic to a little person who has to get stuck. Well, we found out that Jennifer never moved her arm because she didn't want "to hurt the IV" – but mostly because she wouldn't have to get stuck again. I remember the medical people being amazed that the same IV was in there for ten days if not two weeks.

Isn't supposed to last that long, but with her it did, because that was Jennifer, just like that.

When we went to the hospital, we tried almost every time to get a private room for a lot of reasons and, this one time when Jennifer was 10 or so, we happened to have a private room at Lutheran General. Now, one of the key things with CF patients is they have to cough – it's part of the body's cleansing mechanism. She was sick and she just couldn't do what was necessary, so we tried to figure out how the hell we were going to make her laugh because we knew that once she started to laugh, she would start to cough.

Donna: When she and I laugh, we start coughing. So, I knew if I could make her laugh, she's going to cough.

Evan: We're in this private room, and Donna, she looked at me and I looked at her. We knew what we were both thinking, Jennifer's got to laugh, because she's got to cough. Donna stands up and takes her pants down – she moons her daughter.

Evan: Jennifer went ballistic with her laughing and then coughing ... And, at right about that time, the door opens, and in walks the doctor and the residents – must have been four or five of them. And there's Donna with her ass up in the air, with Jennifer going ballistic, and I'm on the floor laughing.

That's what we did, that's how we handled it. Right way? I definitely know it wasn't the wrong way.

Donna: I always knew, if I made her laugh, she'd cough.

Clinical trials?

Evan: Participation in clinical trials was offered over the years, but we never did it. Even when Jennifer became an adult, she turned it down.

We all recognized that the concept of the clinical trial is not for the patient in the trial, it's for those who follow. The odds of a clinical trial working for the patient in the trial is almost nil. Therefore, the word "trial." It's an experiment – that's all it is. Sounds good, but it does no more, no less than if I were to put this drop in this vial to see what happens. Much more sophisticated, but that's basically what it is.

Donna: It's not only that. You don't know if you're getting the placebo or if you're getting the real thing.

Evan: In some trials, that's true. That's very true. Sometimes you don't know.

Support group?

Donna: When Jennifer was first diagnosed, I had lunch with this one lady who had two children with CF, and at the time I think her son had died and her daughter was studying to be a nurse. Then ... the daughter passed away in her 20s. I learned things from this lady because I didn't know myself. But I never wanted to be in a support group, because my daughter was doing okay, as well as she could do, and I didn't want to hear about this one's dying, and this one getting a port ... things like that.

Talk about death

Donna: We never talked about it as a family until she brought it up.

Our approach was ... we gave her information that she could comprehend at each age so, for example, when she was 3, the information was for a 3 year old. Of course, the information got bigger, more expansive as she got older, and we always answered questions truthfully.

I believe she was 10 when she said for the first time, "Am I going to die from Cystic Fibrosis?"

I remember, we were sitting at the kitchen table. I wanted to be truthful, but I also didn't want to make her afraid.

Instead of saying "yes" because I did not believe she would die necessarily, I said that "yes, people do die from Cystic Fibrosis, but that doesn't necessarily mean that you are going to die of Cystic Fibrosis, because we're going to do this, this, this, and this. Everybody has it at a different degree of severity and, with all the things we do to keep you healthy, you're doing great. You need to be as strong as possible, so that when something comes along, you'll be a candidate for it."

We also projected to Jennifer to make sure that she doesn't get near anyone that's sick – "make sure you take care of yourself as well as you can" – and I think that's probably why she became a germophobic.

Sharing information about CF

Jennifer: I did not want anyone to know about my disease. I suppose I just did not want to be perceived as different from everyone else. That was my choice on how to live my CF early years but all that changed as I got older.

Donna: Jennifer never shared information about CF when she was younger. Other than with her close friends – they knew she had something, although they may not have known it was CF. And family members. Family members knew it. She would never hide it with them. It was mostly with people she just met, people that weren't close to her. She might have been embarrassed and didn't want to feel different. I remember when she had to take her pills in a public situation, she would do it in such a way that you never even knew she took them.

Evan: She didn't hide the CF from her close friends, like Lawren or any of her other friends. She didn't hide it – she just acted like what was for her normal. She did whatever needed to be done. She was usually discreet about it, but she did what needed to be done.

You wouldn't know it, but that's what she did. I don't know where that came from? Is it nature or nurture? All I know is, we always tried to make things feel "normal."

As Jennifer got older, I have to say that between her and maybe a couple of her friends she probably talked about it and, if they were over at the house and

Jennifer had to take the medications, there were occasional questions. We would answer them as we answered all questions – matter of factly. We didn't make a big deal out of it. For example, I remember on occasion even doing the postural drainage while one or two of her friends were in the house. Before they could go out to play or whatever, I'd say to Jennifer, "Come on, before you go, let's do the 'act.'" To her 'Oh, dad,' I'd say, 'Come on let's go. It's 10 minutes, we're done.'" So, the kids would know that something was going on, but we didn't make it a big deal – it was just our new normal. Sure, behind the scenes, there were plenty of times that we cried and got crazy, absolutely, but never in front of others.

Sometimes word got out

Jennifer: I remember one time I was in the hospital for an exacerbation and a friend was doing a report and she chose to write about CF. I was mortified and nervous that EVERYONE at school would know why I was in the hospital and then they would know that I had the disease she was reporting on for her school paper. I was very upset and, of course, when I got back to school no one even batted an eye. That was how secretive I was about my disease. I just did not want anyone to know.

Donna: Lisa was her very best friend from when we moved to Deerfield when Jennifer was 5½. Lisa came from a family of ... there were 3 of them, and the mother was ... I don't know what she was doing, but

Lisa didn't really have a mother figure so she was always with me. It was like my second child – they just adored each other, and they were always at my house. Jennifer's friends loved to be at the house because I would make wonderful cakes and feed them.

There was one thing that happened with Lisa. I think Jennifer was at the hospital at the time, and they had some kind of assignment. Lisa wrote about Cystic Fibrosis, and we weren't happy about it because it made reference to Jennifer and now everybody kind of knew.

Evan: That letter, report, whatever Lisa wrote, was the first time that we had to deal with an outside situation. I remember, Donna's right, we were concerned … It didn't feel right.

Donna: It singled her out, and Jennifer didn't want that. She didn't want anyone to know she was different. Like I said before, when she had to take her enzymes before a meal, nobody even knew she took them. That's how quick she was to hide it.

8 – A TEENAGER BLOSSOMS

Jennifer: They were told not to expect their daughter to attend high school. That was in October 1974. They didn't know me or my parents. I got through high school and college, all at the standard pace, and dealt with the ups and downs of hospitalization and sicknesses with a smile on my face. I had very supportive parents and still do to this day!

On dawning of puberty

Evan: When puberty hit, that was an interesting time. We had always been very physical, as you can imagine, and here comes puberty. We used to hug so tight. But, when she began to develop, the hugs became like ... "Okay, don't touch me ... I won't touch you ..." But I respected her and I respected her space. I wasn't going to make her feel uncomfortable or embarrassed or whatever. That lasted until she was about 20, then we could hug again.

Only one confrontation

Evan: I wasn't a dictatorial type of father. That wasn't my style. I never found a need to do that. That's why I always laugh, "Gee, I guess you were listening," because I never sat her down and said, "You have to listen to me."

There was only one confrontation that I can remember between Jennifer and me. Only one. She had to be around 12. It was winter time, and it was right after dinner. Jennifer wasn't home, so I asked "Where's Jennifer?" and Donna answered, "I don't know."

Half an hour, 45 minutes, an hour later – who knows? – here she comes walking in. "Where were you?" I had a good idea where she was, and she lied to me. That's one of the things that I hate most, when people lie. I can handle the truth. I may not like it, but tell me the truth.

I took her and, in an open area, I grabbed her in the winter coat that she was still bundled up in, and I lifted her off the ground. I just kept this kid hanging in the air, and I thought her eyeballs were going to pop out of her head. I never touched her, ever, other than to lift her up.

And that was the end of it. She never lied again, at least that I know. That's how I did it – with firmness, not punishment. That's the way my father treated me. That's how it all came together.

Turning sixteen

Donna: Turning sixteen was an important milestone for Jennifer.

Evan: Sixteen was cool. When she got her license. Now, that was cool. And for her it signified "freedom."

Donna: I gave her a sweet 16 party in my house and served dinner and had a make-up person come.

Jennifer's friends loved to come to my house. The basement was done and we had a ping-pong table, with built in benches all around, and that's where all the kids sat and ate. It was a wonderful party.

Evan: We played a lot of ping-pong. Donna would kill us but Jennifer, when she was little and started learning how to play, she'd make a mistake, hit the ball bad, or whatever, and she'd always say, "Do over, do over ..." So, I'd say, "Okay fine. Do over." Those were the fun times.

Driving lesson

Donna: When we were teaching her how to drive, I took her once. We went to Quill in Lincolnshire – an office supply store that had a gigantic parking lot. I took her and she was driving and I wanted her to put on the break. I kept yelling, "Step on the gas, step on the gas." Of course, I meant the break, and we kept going faster and faster."

Evan: Needless to say, that was the one and only time she took her to teach her how to drive, which is not true, but mostly I taught her. I took her to a similar if not the same parking lot. Her birthday was in January, and I thought it was important for her to understand what a car can and can't do, like on snow or ice or what have you. We went over there. I remember this like it was yesterday. It was a Sunday morning, and it had just snowed. I said, "Okay, take it up to 20 miles an hour and slam on the breaks and let's see what happens."

That's how I taught her, because I believe that's how you teach people by exposing them to what they're going to experience. That is more effective that saying, "If you step on the breaks, you're going to skid." Well, if you've never skidded, how the hell do you know what that is? So she learned how to take it out of the skid.

On the way home, I stopped at a Shell station where most of their businesses is towing. In the back is where they keep the wrecks until the insurance companies come and pick them up. I said, "I just want to show you something." She said, "What are showing me this for?" And I said, "I want to show you what mistakes look like." We looked into one of the cars and, by chance, there was blood all over the place. I said, "Take a good close look at that."

Boyfriends

Donna: She always had a boyfriend, always. She never was without a boyfriend. And she had very long relationships. In fact, the one that was a five-year relationship, I thought she would marry him and that he'd become our son-in-law.

One thing – none of her boyfriends were Jewish, and we're Jewish. But it doesn't matter what you are. I mean, to me everyone is equal and, if you're a good person, you could be any religion, any color, any whatever.

Evan: It is what it is.

First date

Evan: I remember the first date. I remember the kid ... his name was Ricky. Obviously, I'm not tall, but I was 70 pounds heavier then. I remember him coming and standing in the hallway. I shook hands with him. As he was standing there, I kept increasing the pressure on his hand (and in those days, I could tear telephone books). I could see his face changing from, like, "what the hell's going on here?" to "this hurts." I said, "Have her back by 11:00. Have a good time." That's what I said.

Donna: We always worried, not just when she dated, but anytime she left the house. We might have been in bed, but never asleep until we heard the garage door open.

Jennifer Codell

Teen pageant slated for this weekend

Jennifer Codell, daughter of Donna and Evan Codell of Deerfield, has been selected as a semi-finalist in the 1989 Miss Illinois Teen-USA Pageant which will take place this weekend in the grand ballroom f the Woodfield Hilton Hotel. Tne winner will represent Illinois in the 1989 Miss Teen-USA Pageant, which will be televised live in July.

Codell is a junior at Stevenson High School where she is on the honor roll and has won awards in tennis and softball.

It was the normal fear that any parent has with a teenager – not because of CF. It's not like a disease where you go out, you're okay but, within an hour or two, you could be bad.

Evan: For the most part, we organized our schedule around hers. As she got older, we had less control. Of course, she had to go on dates. Of course, she had to go out with her buddies. We just did what we had to do around Jennifer's activities.

There were times when we had to say, "No, you can't go," because of health-related issues. But she would still want to go – my god, she was a teenager.

Aspects of boy relationships

Evan: In some of Jennifer's young romances, CF had an impact there. I remember her saying, "He broke up with me because I have CF." This is probably the first time where CF had a major interference in her life – that because of CF, something happened. I think that might have been the first time, other than minor instances like, "You can't go, you got a cold." To me, that was minor. This was major. The boy wasn't mature enough, possibly, or brave enough, to accept Jennifer and her Cystic Fibrosis.

Donna: I don't remember her being devastated or anything, like, real bad. Do you?

Evan: She had 24 hours to deal with it, then let's move on. It's what I taught her.

Donna: She never had trouble getting boyfriends. I mean, she had a boyfriend all the time.

Evan: She was a good-looking girl. She had a great body. She was smart.

I remember one time ... I had a speed bag in the basement of our townhouse a speed bag, and I taught her how to hit it. I remember some guy came over and bet her $10 that she couldn't do it ... and she got the 10 bucks – she loved it like her mother.

She loved to show people up. Especially men, just like her mother. Loved it.

Donna: Absolutely. Are you kidding? When I play tennis, I'm in favor of beating the guys. One guy said to me, "One day, Donna ..." So, I say, "I've been playing for 40 years. You've been playing for a year. Give me a break."

Evan: Bring it on.

Donna: Bring it on.

High school graduation

Evan: She graduated from Stevenson High School, and that was a great day. We were very proud of her, and you could see how proud she was of herself as she did it. She was beautiful. She was healthy. She looked good. She felt good. It was a good time. Hotter than hell that day, I remember that, at Ravinia. It was just a beautiful day. But

mostly it was just a day of pride. Even my mother was there. I mean, maybe you could tell more. I don't know.

Donna: You know what? I don't even remember.

Evan: It's interesting how we remember different things, or the same things, but differently.

Donna: I think maybe I thought that her graduation from high school meant she would be leaving to go to college.

Choosing a college

Evan: There was a boy involved in Jennifer's college choice.

Donna: That's right, her boyfriend, Lawren, was at Eastern. I don't think there was ever a question. She was going to Eastern.

Evan: All those other things that kids think about, with Jennifer it was the boy. He was a year older, I think. A year to two.

Donna: They went together for five years. We were very close with him and his family. He was the one who broke up. When he did that, he wrote me a letter. He was so afraid that I'd be angry at him.

Evan: That happened when she was still in college, because after Lawren was Jack. And it was after Jack that she finally met Mark, who became her husband.

9 – YOUNG WOMAN FLIES FROM NEST

Jennifer: When I was a young adult, my life was all about school and how I could get through college while being around people who might be sick in the classroom. I had to maintain a social life and still be compliant with my care. I was able to stay compliant and get through college in only four years! As an adult going into the corporate world, I had more control about avoiding "sick" people or so I thought. I again found it hard to stay away from people who were sick. I found my own health declining and had to make the hard decision to take a disability retirement.

Dreams for the future

Evan: Jennifer had dreams about graduation and life after college. Because of the way she was brought up, she never thought of her CF as a terminal condition. We all assumed she would live a full life, whatever the hell that means. You can't do that to your child – you can't take away dreams even if they're unrealistic. It would be cruel to do that.

Filled with hope

Evan: Jennifer blossomed as an adult, literally. Like all kids do, especially women, she blossomed. And she used everything we taught her – I guess she was listening. She was engaging. She was fun to be with. She made people around her feel better than they did before she met them. Maya Angelou has a quote, "People will forget what you said, and people will forget what you did, but they will never forget how you made them feel." That was Jennifer. And she was extremely ambitious, extremely organized, extremely goal-orientated, extremely empathetic and compassionate. She was filled with hope.

Leaving home

Evan: One of the hardest times for us was when she went away to school because we literally had no knowledge of what was going on. She went to Eastern Illinois in Charleston – I just hoped and prayed that all the hard work that Donna and I put into it carried over into Jennifer.

Staying in touch

Donna: During her college years, we stayed in pretty close touch. Well, for sure once a week we talked on the phone. Then, of course, if she needed money, she'd call me sooner. And she came home for every holiday. We went there for whatever was going on – Parent's Weekend or whatever.

Evan: Back then, it wasn't like it is now with cellphones and all the rest. We talked when we could. We went down there, but we didn't force ourselves.

Donna: Whenever she would call needing money, she was direct, saying, "Mom, I need some money." I would respond, "Bad connection, bad connection. I can't hear you."

Evan: Did we hear from her frequently? As weird as it sounds, when the answer is no, we kind of took it as a positive. Why? Because if you didn't hear, that means things were rolling along, that there were no crises where the parent needed to be involved.

Our last family trip

Donna: I think our favorite vacation was at Marco Island.

Evan: That was our last family trip.

Donna: Jennifer was in college – I think it was between her junior and senior year. The three of us went, and it's an island where if it rains, there's nothing to do, and it rained. On the way there, on the plane, they gave us some food, and I'm the only one who ate sausage on the plane ... and I got food poisoning.

We got to the hotel, and I just was sick as a dog. I didn't go out to dinner. They went ... whatever ... and, after they got back, I was feeling sick and had to head to the bathroom, but you needed to put a card in the thing, and it didn't work, and I'm yelling at Jennifer to put the card in. Well, of course we all started laughing because we laughed at everything, and we finally got the card to work.

Another funny little story is when we played tennis there. It was clay, and clay is slippery. And Jennifer is doing an overhead, and falls flat on her behind. So, once again, we laugh. Hysterical.

Progress through college

Evan: Amazingly, Jennifer graduated college in four years. Even under normal conditions, with no health issues, to have a child in her day, or even today, get out of school in four years is not as common as it used to be. And Jennifer with good grades – B, B+, and higher. That's with hospitalization at least once a year, when she was out of school for maybe as long as a month.

Now, missing a month of college? Holy shit. How do you make that up? It's not like eighth grade where you got a workbook. She did it.

Amazing. I mean, who does that? Who wouldn't give in? It was so easy to give up at that age. But, for Jennifer, failure was not an option. That was Jennifer.

Jennifer graduated high school on time. She went to college, and she graduated in four years. Each year she was sick, and she still graduated. What does that tell you about a human being?

To whom

My name is Jennifer and I am one of many young adults that suffer from a chronic lung disease called Cystic Fibrosis. I recently learned that a Bill might be passed to stop Orphan Drug use. I only wish + hope that the bill to stop this will not go thru. My life + others lives depend on these studies that are done w/ Orphan Drugs. The only way to find a cure for my disease lies w/ the chance of using orphan drugs to experiment + find a cure. I realize to do all this it takes money, a alot of it. There's always government spend for military which has been the most spend by the govt in the most recent years. You spend money so our military will have the right equipment *so they can battle if they have to + win. Well we're fighting along w/ others w/ c.f. our own Battle & to win our war we need the right equipment. This equipement comes from the orphan drug program which helps researches find a cure that will win + conquer the Cystic Fibrosis battle Please help us win our fight. ——*

Work as a consultant

Evan: After Jennifer graduated from college, she went to work for Hewitt and Associates. She was there less than a year, unfortunately. It was her Cystic Fibrosis that caused her to leave. The workload was humongous, and she just couldn't do it. She was smart enough, but physically she couldn't handle it – it was too demanding. At the time, Hewitt was famous for working these kids into the ground – with demands of 60, 80 hours a week.

Diabetes sets in

Donna: When Jennifer was in her late 20s, she developed diabetes, which is totally common for adults with CF but we didn't know that at first.

Evan: For adult CF patients, because of the way the disease works, the pancreas which regulates so many things in our body is affected by CF and the mucus. For a lot of CF adults over the years, the pancreas feels attacked constantly and can't produce the insulin needed so it's called on-set diabetes.

Donna: Well, they didn't used to know much about that because kids didn't live long enough to develop diabetes.

Evan: As CF people started living longer, this ugly thing raised its head.

Donna: It presented a problem because with Cystic Fibrosis you have to eat a high fat meal, and with diabetes you have to eat a low fat meal, so they bumped heads. What she was told is go with the high fat meal and regulate the insulin with shots.

Evan: As Donna mentioned earlier, when she would take her enzymes, when she was old enough to administer it for herself, she would do it in such a way that, unless you were paying close attention, you wouldn't know. She carried that practice forward with her insulin shots. We'd be out let's say at a restaurant, and we'd finish our meal, and I would notice that she'd lift up her shirt ...

Donna: Squeezed her belly, and put a shot in there.

Evan: Goodbye. You would never know.

Treatment for CF over the years

Donna: With Cystic Fibrosis today, things are different. For one, 10% of Cystic Fibrosis patients have a mutated gene that allows them to take one particular medicine that offers great benefits. Jennifer didn't have that gene. Also, the treatments and the medicines are much more advanced than when Jennifer was diagnosed, so I think kids have a better chance now.

Evan: To expand on that, today we live in a world of information, and there's so much more available today that is so easy to get to. Back in '74, all you had basically was written material published by doctors. Today, the internet provides access to so much more. But it's a double-edge sword. You go into the internet now, and it literally is one of the scariest places ever. It's a wealth of knowledge, yes, with many things we would've benefited from, but also at the same time it would have scared the hell out of us.

Donna: If I ask myself, is there anything that I know now that I wish I knew in those early years? I'd come out, I think, with no. I think we did everything that we could have done and more, and we knew everything there was to know because we made sure we did. If there was a new medication, whatever. There weren't too many new discoveries when she was growing up. Things got better in 1989 when the gene was found, but really for those 17 years treatment options stayed pretty much the same.

Evan: I agree with Donna on that. I don't believe in second guessing, it's a waste of time. I refer to it as mental masturbation. It does nobody any good. Did I do everything correctly? No. Did I make a mistake? Yes. But I'll tell you this, nothing was ever done without the best of intentions. Circumstances, age, education, intelligence, that all goes into the equation and, given all that, I believe that Donna and I did a hell of a job. I'm not patting myself on the back because as I said earlier the proof was in the pudding. Jennifer was the pudding. There's no way on this God's earth that she would have ended up like she did without us.

Taking care of herself

Evan: Jennifer was so careful in everything that she did when it came to taking care of herself. Whether it was the insulin, the Inhalation therapy, the postural drainage. When she became an adult, a vest was developed that vibrated when you plugged into the wall, put it on like a ski-jacket.

She was so careful, not only in the administration of all these treatments, but also doing them as normally as brushing your teeth. That was her normal. She never said, "Ah, to hell with it," like so many CF adults do. Why? Because she didn't know how to quit, that's why.

Crazy for cleanliness

Evan: And she was crazy about cleanliness.

Donna: She was nuts about it.

Evan: She was off the charts. She took it to the extreme, and that's fine. It worked for her.

Rare glimpse of Jennifer's anger

Evan: I think the most I ever saw Jennifer get upset was at Donna.

Donna: I wanted her to take my product, which is Juice Plus. It's fruits and vegetables in a capsule, a soft chewable. Very well researched, and there are 36 peer-reviewed studies published in leading medical journals. It has literally saved people's lives. My husband is still here, and I believe it's because of that.

Evan: I say it's part of the equation.

Donna: Right. Another doctor that is a colleague of mine, he had the "widow-maker" heart attack in 2010, and he said Juice Plus saved his life. He's still here, too.

Evan: We don't need a commercial for Juice Plus.

Donna: I know, but I'm leading up to ... excuse me ... I wanted Jennifer to take my product.

Evan: Jennifer and Mark wouldn't accept anything we said. We gave them everything to study. So, they ask, "Who pays for the studies?" If they could find a reason not to do it, they did.

Donna: None of my friends could understand why she wouldn't try it. I'd say, "Give it a try for four months. Give it a try, because there's an orchard and a garden blend. Then, they came out with a vineyard blend, which makes a big difference because three that work synergistically together. We even brought a box to her to take, and we went home with it, because she was not going to take it. She and I, over the last four years of her life, had this conflict with Juice Plus to the degree that I would cry hysterically and she would hang up the phone on me.

Evan: It drove me insane.

Donna: She would be screaming at the top of her lungs, which made me feel horrible, because I didn't want to aggravate her, or make her feel bad, but I loved her so much ...

Evan: The bottom line is this, and I said this, and it still upsets me today, as you clearly can see. Donna, make a choice, Juice Plus or your daughter. That's your choice. Don't give me any bullshit about studies and what it may or may not do.

Donna: She once made the comment to me, "I want my mother back."

Evan: There's your answer. That's amazing, it still upsets me to this day. I never – after that one time when I went to their house, and I pleaded my case with regard to the Juice Plus – I never mentioned it again.

Donna: I promised I wouldn't … and then of course, I did, because I always wanted to make things better, and I thought that it could make things better.

Mark enters, Jennifer exits

Donna: Jennifer met Mark at Bally's in …

Evan: Deerfield.

Donna: … Deerfield. It's a gym, was a gym. Mark was manager, and Jennifer came home and told me that she met a guy that's eleven years older than her and has a three-year old. "Stay away from him," I said. That's all I had to say. She was going to fix him up with our neighbor. They all went out, but Mark didn't want the neighbor, he wanted Jennifer.

   So, they started dating, and she comes home one day and tells me she's going to move in with him. She proceeds to start taking her clothes, and putting them in trash bags to take to the car.

Evan: I come home from work, and I see these garbage bags at the foot of the stairs. "What's going on?" Jennifer proceeds to tell me she's moving in with Mark. I went crazy. Even to this day it bothers me. I spent the next two hours at least in the basement with her, trying to convince her not to do this. To her credit, she stood her ground, said, "It's what I'm doing." I tried to think of every reason not to do it. Some made sense, some made absolutely no sense, but I used everything in my quiver. At the end of that two hours, whatever, I was dead meat, I had no place to go, and she proceeded to finish loading up her car.

Donna: And she got angry that we weren't helping her.

Evan: I said to her, "Why would I help you if I disagree with your decision?" You see I didn't want her to be hurt. I didn't know Mark intimately, I was concerned about CF and her health, even though she had spent four years on her own in college. That rope I talk about – it was pretty much unwound when Jennifer went away to school. Now the rope was gone. It was very emotional, very disturbing, and it was done in such a way that I thought at the time, and I do believe even to this day, that it was disrespectful to the two of us, the way she handled it.

As much as Donna and I have tried to paint a very positive picture of Jennifer as a human being, she wasn't perfect – far from it. She was human. That being said, I felt that we should have talked about it. Not in a way that there was an ultimatum. Not in a way that "I already made my mind up, I don't give a shit what you say." Not in a way of "I'm in the process of moving out."

What if I hadn't come home? What if I was at an appointment, or I was delayed, whatever? She would have been gone. That's what I'm talking about. I thought at the time, and I still do, that it was disrespectful, that I always tried in my own way to be respectful of her feelings, and I didn't think she was respectful of ours. She let us down – something she really never ever did. Certainly not at this level. This was the most disappointing time ...

10 – MARRIAGE COMPLETES JENNIFER

Jennifer: Who motivates me you ask? Three words: My husband, Mark! Mark is why I do it all. Mark is why I want to be around till I am old and gray! Mark is my everything! What happens to me, happens to Mark. 1 Corinthians 13:4 pretty much says a lot of what my Mark means to me and what he does for me on a daily basis. " ... Love always protects, always trusts, always hopes, always perseveres."

Child rearing philosophy

Evan: I have a silly theory with regard to raising and rearing children – a theory I've maintained forever – and it goes like this. When a child is born, if you can remember how tightly you held your baby, now I want you to envision that you have a rope wrapped around the baby. The end of the rope was in your hand. In the initial stages, that rope is very tight. There's not much room between you and the baby. Therefore, the length of the rope is very short. Assuming everything is normal, as the child grows, you let out some of the rope. They start to crawl, you're going to have to let the rope out. They start to walk, you have to let the rope out some more. They go to school, they get on the bus for the first time, you have to let the rope out. As long as you hold the end of the rope, you still have a semblance of control. When necessary, you can pull on that

rope and let them know you're still there. That continues over their life to the point where at some point, it's
time to let go of the rope. It's different for everybody.
With Jennifer, it was when she got married. I said,
"Now you're on your own," and I let go of the rope.
The feelings didn't go away, but the concept of control,
at whatever level, was gone.

Marriage to Mark

Evan: Jennifer's marriage to Mark ... I look at it and say,
"It was the best thing that ever happened to Jennifer,"
and I mean that abso-
lutely.

Donna: I've told Mark
countless times how
much we love him for
what he did with
Jennifer, and took care
of her, and he re-
sponded to me saying
it wasn't just him tak-
ing care of her, she
took care of him.

Evan: I'm glad you brought that up because you are
100% right. Jennifer was not this little flower, just sitting there, going "Oh, honey," bullshit. She took care of
business, and she made him a different human being.
For one thing, she brought him out of his shell. She basically convinced him that he's a good person, that he's
a real man. She made him a better human being. She

opened his eyes. As much as Mark brought to the table, I have to say that Jennifer was equal in what she brought to the marriage.

Donna: He would tell you that.

Evan: They had something in their marriage that most people who are married would give their eye teeth for. That was the kind of relationship that they had. It was strong on so many levels, not just physical, sexual, sensual, financial, spiritual – it was on every level that you can think of. They were in step with one another. I think you would be hard-pressed to find many couples that can say that truthfully. They each brought equal amounts to the table, both positive and negative, but they came away with much more positive than negative. That's what I think.

How Mark helped

Donna: One big way that Mark was helpful is he wasn't a worry wart like we are.

Evan: Yeah, you're right.

Donna: You take care of the situation when it happens. You don't worry what's going to happen down the line. He helped her to be strong. To not worry about tomorrow, but take care of what is today.

Evan: We're on the same page with that. She used to refer to him as "my rock." Those were her words, "Mark is my rock," and she was right. We appreciated Mark very much, and loved him, for how he took care of our child.

We knew, when the marriage time came, she was in good hands with Mark. With the way they conducted their lives. Did we agree with everything? Absolutely not, but we never said a word. I told Jennifer once, "The only time I would say anything is if I saw you ready to fall off a cliff. Then I'd get involved. Or if you asked my opinion. Without those two things, it's your life. Knock your socks off." We never interfered.

Another thing I made her aware of ... Mark had a son from his first marriage. At the time, Quentin was, I don't know, four years old, three years old. I told her, based on my own experience, "Don't put Mark in a position of having to choose between Quentin and you, because you will lose 100% of the time." She got it. Unfortunately, she never had a good relationship with Quentin, but she understood.

But Mark is a remarkable human being. I remember having lunch with him one day, and he had just gone to the doctor with Jennifer. He told me that the main purpose of the visit was for him to ask questions.

Donna: Before they decided to get married, she wanted to take him to the doctor to show him what he was getting into.

Evan: Again, that's Jennifer. Who else would think of that stuff?

In a nutshell ...

Evan: When I think about our relationship with Mark, let me sum it up this way. It's not about me. It's not about Donna. It's about Jennifer. As long as Jennifer was safe and comfortable and taken care of and following what we thought was the right way to live, I didn't care. I wasn't looking for a son, I wasn't looking for a friend, I was wanting to have someone take care of Jennifer, and that's what Mark did.

Becoming a mother?

Donna: I think Jennifer wanted a child very badly, and never really expressed that but made a wise decision between her and her husband not to have a child.

Evan: She didn't consult us. It was her and Mark. Could she physically? Yes. Practically? Big mistake. But we didn't say to her, "Yes" or "No." Also, she didn't ask and I made it a practice that, unless she asked, I didn't say a word. She never asked, so I never said a word.

Donna: I would never bring it up because it was a sore spot. I mean, it was a sore spot to me – that I would never be a grandma, so I certainly wasn't going to bring up to her that she would never be a mother.

Evan: Oh, absolutely.

Jennifer: We had to deal with the decision to have children or not. It was a big decision to think I will never be called mommy. It sometimes really pulls at my heart strings. My husband and I decided my health was too important and high maintenance, and to have a child would be too hard for us. That was our decision for and what was right for our lives. Now, it is just Mark, me, and CF which is kind of like a baby. It does require lots of care, daily feedings and tons of attention!

Going to Florida

Evan: Jennifer was 38 or 39 when they moved to Florida - it was really just the last four or five years she was down there. They both wanted to go to Florida, but the reason they didn't go earlier is because of Mark's son, Quentin – they wanted him to graduate high school before they left.

Donna: So, they waited.

Evan: When it happened, it was just like it was when she moved out of our house – "I'm going to Florida – bye!" Right. There was no, "Hey, dad, we're thinking of moving to Florida. What do you think?" But that's what I raised, so I can't complain. I gave her the ability to do that.

11 – THE BEST YEARS

Jennifer: I am enjoying Florida and just looking out at the beach and the open water really speaks to my soul. My need to talk about my CF and make people aware of what I go through and to share ideas with other people with CF has increased. I found I enjoy talking to people about my CF experience and even more I enjoy talking with others who have CF or whose loved ones have CF.

The best thing

Donna: Jennifer loved Florida.

Evan: Oh, my god, it was the best thing to ever happen to her.

Donna: Best five years of her life. Just loved it. Loved the warmth of it. Started paddle boarding. Bike riding. Just doing it all ... In Florida, where they lived, every Friday night there was a band that would play. I mean, there was just so many things to do.

Evan: She was born for that, and they took advantage of it all. We stayed in touch regularly with texts and emails and Skype.

Donna: I never felt she was totally gone because I could always see her on Skype.

CEO of my health

Evan: For the last couple of years of her life I would say, probably 40-50% of her waking day was spent in taking care of herself. When people first met her and asked, "What do you do?" she would say, "I'm Chief Executive Officer of me."

Donna: Of my health. "I am CEO of my health."

Jennifer: Dealing with insurance companies is as frustrating as a bad itch on your back that you cannot reach. Now, not only am I an adult dealing with a terminal disease but also handling all the paperwork, insurance companies, doctor appointments …

Now my "JOB" is me and taking care of myself so I can stay as healthy as possible. The problem is that I cannot fire myself! I have to keep going and doing all the meds and therapies. My advancement is not promotions, raises, or a different job description. My promotion is being able to get through the night without sleeping on five pillows, getting out to the gym on a regular basis, ordering meds and supplies, and doing all my therapies and medications on schedule.

The disability stereotype

Donna: One day, Jennifer was at the gym, and she had her oxygen strapped on of course, and one of the gals didn't know how to use a certain machine, so she went over to Jennifer and asked her, "How do you do this?" The other friend with her says, "You've got to be kidding. Of all the people there to ask, you pick someone who's on oxygen to tell you how to use the machine?"

The truth is she was probably the best person to ask –
she always wanted to help people. No matter what.

---

*Jennifer: With my oxygen (O_2) tank in tow, I set up my bike
the other day to start Spin class. Setting up is a process of adjusting the seat, the handle bars and resistance. Along with
wiping the bike down with sanitary wipes and then setting up
my O_2 tank so it does not fall, Gatorade goes in the drink spot
and a towel is kept handy. I have found that just hanging my O_2
tank bag on the handle bars works best for me ...*

*Well, the class was almost over the other day and the instruc-
tor was walking up and down the aisles chanting her motivational words of wisdom when she stopped by me and pointed to
her nose and asked me, in the middle of class, on her microphone, why I have the oxygen. I thought I would be mortified
but, really, it was my chance to say why and then people can
move on and not look at me and wonder. Although, I am sure
no one was even paying attention. But when something is different about us, I think we all feel self-conscious to some degree,
because we all just want to be accepted for who we are. Right!*

*So, I tell her I have Cystic Fibrosis and only a 40% lung ca-
pacity. She says in the microphone how I am her hero and how
strong I am – yadda, yadda, yadda. Then the guy next to me
starts nodding his head in agreement. I thought I was going to
fall off my bike. My feet were fastened into the shoe straps so
that would have been impossible. Ha, ha! But, really, I was relieved and now it was not such an elephant in the room.*

*Again, her reaction was fantastic ... People say how strong I
am, but I do not feel that what I am doing is strong. I feel it just
is what I have to do to stay healthy.*

New friends

Donna: It's funny how things turn out – the girl who said, "Of all the people to ask ..." became Jennifer's very best friend. Her name was Kate. She was having a rough time dealing with certain things, and she told me, "Jennifer was always there to help me no matter what. No matter how she felt, no matter what." They had a certain group of girls – there were three of four of them – and every Thursday night they would go out to eat. If they couldn't go out to eat because Jennifer didn't feel good, they'd bring the food to her.

She also told me that they were going to clean Jennifer's house when she got the transplant. My daughter had a phobia with germs, and everything had to be so clean. So, while she was out getting her transplant, they were going to come and clean the house. Everything was set up for when the time came.

Jennifer: Being 40 with CF, I have been around the block and to give hope to families whose small children have CF has been one of my greatest accomplishments. I now love talking about CF with people and sharing my story and experiences. It is a far cry from what I used to be like growing up, but this hope that I can share with others is sometimes just what that other person needs and that is a great feeling.

There are a couple of chat rooms and forums to peruse in the CF community and I have actually met some really great people who I now talk to not only on the forum but also via phone. It has been great to share our stories, experiences and even laugh at some of the things CF people go through. It is really comforting to talk to someone who "gets it" and who has been through the same things I have, as well as things I haven't experienced. I get their honest opinion and first-hand experience of a medication, procedure, or therapy and that is priceless information. Yes, the doc can explain things thoroughly but the doc has not gone through it and "felt" it, so it is nice to ask my friends in the CF community what the real deal is.

Since we cannot be physically around someone with CF, having these places to go is a great alternative. It is a place where you can ask any question about what you're dealing with and you will get all kinds of responses. Some good, some bad, and some that make you really think. It is a good resource to have at your fingertips and that is exactly how I use it - as a resource. I love that some people have emerged to become great friends and that is a bonus! The days of CF camps are over so now we have virtual camps and for the teens out there that is really a great thing. I know some people out there don't have a lot of support in their CF journey and these forums can provide support for them.

12 – HEALTH DECLINES

Jennifer: I will never forget the words coming out of my doctor's mouth back in February 2015. My doctor said, "It is time to start the listing process and get listed for a double lung transplant." I did not ask for this disease that is slowly killing me and robbing me of the very breath that I need to sustain my life. This substance is suffocating me and slowly robbing me of my existence on this Earth. I will not go down without a fight. Like an amateur boxer going 15 excruciating rounds against the World Champ, can I answer the bell one more time? I will do what I can to stave off this dreadful disease. I will look to the ocean for my strength and look to my husband for the love and courage to keep fighting. I have wonderful support from my husband and family but, in the end, it is up to me!

Likelihood of transplant

Evan: You can never know really how close you are getting to a lung transplant. They don't give you that information. There are a zillion variables that determine suitability of a match – body type, blood type, whatever. In our discussions, we never got beyond the transplant itself. We talked about what the surgery would be like, what recuperation would look like. We never talked about whether it would work or not. We assumed it would because that's what we do.

The waiting begins

Jennifer: As I have been waiting to get the call for new lungs, I thought how similar it is to waiting on the tarmac when stuck in a plane. How similar it is to see the gate (my new lungs) and to know it is right there and you can walk there faster than it would take for this airplane to get the all-clear to taxi to the gate. Waiting for the call to come for new lungs, waiting for life to begin again, waiting for a second chance, waiting and waiting ...

So, you ask me or wonder how is it I wait? How is it I go on in a state of health that is so very hard to endure? A simple shower leaves me out of breath, and let's not even talk about stairs. Stairs are my nemesis. I am so out of breath from walking upstairs, it is exhausting. I am so tired of being out of breath. But this is my cross to bear, this is my life right now and I will endure until that phone rings with the miracle of more life. Until my "gate" is ready, I will wait in a holding pattern for the phone to ring.

I feel God is preparing me for this journey. When I was first told I needed a transplant, it was a very hard reality to accept. Yes, I was on oxygen, and yes, my lung function was low, but I felt I could live this way. I think we as CF people tend to really accept our limitations and live with them and build a life around them. Our "normal" really is not normal at all. So, I have found it hard to realize my normal is far from it. God has shown in me this acceptance of needing a lung transplant. He has helped me come to terms and be able to say, "Okay, I am ready. Let the phone ring and let's do this," because I have a lot more living to do! He has brought people into my life in person,

*via e-mail and via Facebook who have shown me such support
and prayers that I get tears in my eyes just thinking of it all.*

*God is by my side and preparing my path - a path to greatness
and freedom: freedom from being trapped in my body like I am
right now, freedom to do good while I have this time on earth,
freedom to be with my loved ones, freedom to just make dinner
at night or grocery shop, freedom for the little things in life.*

*I am waiting on the tarmac, I am waiting for the call. I can see
it. I can visualize my recovery and fight to get back to what will
be the new me! The gate or I should say my lungs are right there
and I can just see it. But I will be patient. I will settle into my
life that I have now and I will wait for the miraculous phone
call.*

Evan: I know Jennifer would have done everything in
her power to make it work, but she never got that
opportunity.

13 – NOW DAD NEEDS HELP

Jennifer: You gotta keep moving forward with a smile on your face, no matter how much you want to frown. Be an example for all those to see. Be the light that stays on even in the darkest of moments. Keep fighting your battle with a light heart, a smile on your face, and a spark in your eye. This will feed your soul and spirit and give you strength to battle on.

New diagnosis in family

Evan: After I got sick, I never wore the t-shirt that says, "I have cancer." Never. I never liked to wear it on my sleeves. People don't need to know. But Donna is different, and sometimes I get upset with her. I hear her on the phone with some random somebody, "Oh, my husband has cancer." What are you telling them for? What difference does it make? But that's me.

Déjà vu?

Evan: At the time that we learned of Jennifer's CF diagnosis, and even for a while afterwards, it felt like it was a dream. It was like, "This is not real," and those same feelings came to me at my own diagnosis of stage 4 lung cancer. "Wait a minute," I thought. Even though I knew there was something wrong with me several months prior to the diagnosis, still it was like, "Wait a minute ... this is not right."

A competitive spirit

Evan: I grew up in a competitive environment, where the attitude was that you never gave up. That's what I learned. So, Donna and I are both very competitive people. More times than not, that manifested itself somewhere in sports, and also with me and my business, or used to be.

When we were confronted with a situation, we took it as a challenge. A competitive challenge, where there's a winner and there's a loser. And I like to win. I think that attitude has served us well. Like Donna said, we're not going to lose to this. There's no way.

Just as a sidelight, when I got diagnosed, in essence they said, "you'll be lucky if you're here in 6 months. That was 4½ years ago and, last I checked, I am not gone yet. Right now, unfortunately, things are not good, but I haven't lost that will. I've never given up and, more importantly, Jennifer never gave up.

Letting Jennifer know

Evan: Calling Jennifer to tell her I was sick was one of the hardest things I ever had to do, and she took it like a trooper. It was unbelievable to me.

Donna: When we found out, I called Mark at work. I didn't want to tell Jennifer over the phone, but what are we going to do? Take a plane to tell her? No way I could do that. So, I called Mark at work, and I said, "Mark, you have to go home to be with Jennifer. I have to tell her that her father has lung cancer," and he agreed. He was walking in the door as I called to talk with her.

I hardly never referred to Evan as "Daddy" – but I said to Jennifer when she got on the phone, "Daddy ... was diagnosed with lung cancer." She didn't take it very well. It was very hard for her. But Mark was right there for her.

Jennifer: I remember the day clearly. It was spring in Florida and I was at the pool soaking up rays. But oddly, as I looked toward the gate to the pool, I see my husband walking in on a work day in the middle of the afternoon, just as I was talking to mom on my cell phone and she begins to say to me, "Daddy has cancer." What? What? From that moment on our lives changed forever ... I will never forget those three words. "Daddy has cancer." Like me, who has the worst gene makeup for Cystic Fibrosis, he as the worst case of Stage 4 lung cancer. It's a sad and sadistic joke the world has played on us affecting both my lungs and my dad's lungs.

Evan: They were together when Donna called Jennifer. Her first reaction was something like, "Okay, so where are we going now?"

After that initial reaction, from that point on for the most part, all of the conversations between Jennifer and me, whether we were talking about her health, or my health, they were amazingly positive. They were realistic but positive.

Donna: The two of them – Evan and Jennifer – became very close during this period after he got sick, because she was trying to help him.

Jennifer's letter

Dad,

This email might ramble, so bear with me. Do not waste your time going back in your mind, what you could have done differently to make this outcome turn out differently. That is a waste of time and precious energy. Regret is as useful as trying to stop a flooding river with your hands. It will keep you busy but you will still drown. Nobody can go back in time, and we all wish we have done things differently in our lives, but by thinking about it, and wishing about it, it does not change the situation, so why go there? All your energy needs to focus on the now. Focus on what you can do now. Think of the serenity prayer:

"God, grant me the serenity, peace of mind, to accept the things I cannot change, courage to change the things I can, and the wisdom to know the difference."

Take this time to mourn this scary diagnosis, and on Thursday, when you get the game-plan, whatever that might be, you fight.

You are not a quitter, and you did not raise me to be one. I learned it from you, so you have it in you. You think positive. Find the light in the situation no matter how insignificant it might be. You find it and you focus on that. A lot of our health and well-being is directly related to the health of our minds, and you stay positive through this. You fight this with all of your might, and laugh, and smile. Yeah, it is a scary situation, but you can get through this. Head on, plow through, no prisoners. You can control your emotions, and you can pick and choose how you react and act.

Just because a problem forms does not mean it has to prosper. You can deal with this, and you can deal with it in a way that is noble, full of life, and love, and laughter, and meet it head on. Think Rocky (theme song here, da-da-da-da). You are one attitude away from your success. You can have a positive frame of mind and a good attitude to make it through a bad situation. You are strong in mind and body, and don't forget that. Being positive will help get through the tough times. Hang on to every sliver of hope and focus on that.

It is not about learning how to survive a storm, but learning to dance in the rain. It is pouring now, but you have to smile because there is a rainbow, and you concentrate on that. You will find your rainbow no matter what the prognosis and treatment is. A rainbow will emerge, and be appropriate for you only. Remember every passing minute as a chance to turn it all around. Like I said, mourn for now, get your anger out, because come Thursday, and we know what it is, you are out of the gate fighting, turning it around, and if each minute you have to say to yourself, I've got to turn this around, then that is what you do.

Each minute you can start over on a positive track. Take it day by day or hour by hour. Do not think what if, there are no what ifs, there is only what is, and you deal with it as it is presented. The mind cannot handle all the what if scenarios. You have to compartmentalize it, and deal with each little step. Rome was not built in a day. Baby steps forward. I am here for you and I love you very much. You need me, I am there on a plane to you. You can also just stare at each other on Skype, or watch a TV program together on Skype.

Just being there and not saying anything is sometimes needed. You saved me from the alligators, and I wish I could save you from this. Whatever way I can, I will. You fight. You've got a fighter mentality with this, look it straight in the eye and say, *you do not own me, you do not have me. My body may be broken, but my mind is not, and my body will heal. Medicine and technology has advanced, and it is wondrous what they can do now. Who is they, as you would say. One step at a time, one day at a time, one minute at a time. Just put your boxing gloves on because round one is coming. Go champ. You are strong in body, you are strong in mind, you control your emotions and nobody else. You lift yourself up, you conquer. You control how you will react and act. I love you very much.*

Love, Jennifer

Evan: That email I got from Jennifer. That's something. In her words. Not mine, not Donna's.

Donna: It sounded almost like it was you talking.

Evan: I taught Jennifer: When you run into a problem, you have 24 hours to deal with it, and then you have to move on. You can hear that same thing in her words. The only thing I have to say about her email is this – When Jennifer gave me advice using basically the same words that I gave her through life, I thought, "I guess you were listening."

This is a remarkable woman who can say things like this. This is a special human being.

Being Sick Together

Evan: She came out more as she got older. After I got sick, we used to talk a lot during the day and, more times than that, we used to watch "Ellen" together because it made us both laugh. When you watch her show, you got to walk away with a smile on your face unless you're an idiot.

We would laugh over that or we would text or we would talk and text. In the last year, she cried more than I. She cried.

I remember her telling me in the last few months how difficult it was for her to take a shower, and I would sit there and would think to myself, "What are you talking about? All you got to do is stand there. Go like that, dry yourself off, ba-ding, ba-doom, you're done." But I never said anything other than, "I understand. I'm sorry you've got to go through this." Now, with me, it got to the point where I now can't take a shower. I have to sit down on a stool. I have to wear my oxygen. Donna's got to be there. Like we said earlier, until you do it, you have no idea. Now I get it.

Towards the end, I know that Mark would wash Jennifer because she couldn't. They had a loft and the master bedroom suite and another bedroom. The rest of their townhouse is on the first floor. She couldn't walk up the stairs. So, he would carry her up the stairs to take a shower. Mark is a big man, strong, very athletic. She weighed maybe 105 pounds at best, 110 maybe. He'd just pick her up and walk her up the stairs. Never said nothing. Made it like brushing your teeth.

Donna: She never told me this.

Evan: Now you know.

Donna: ... because she knew how I would take it and she wouldn't want to hurt me.

Evan: That's the good thing about having two parents, is that your relationship should be different with each parent. We both bring, as all parents do, hopefully our strength and our positivity to the table, and Jennifer could take the best of our both.

Love you through it

Donna: Jennifer also sent me an email. Her subject was, "Words for You." It was March 30, 2012.

Evan: Right after I got diagnosed.

Jennifer: Here are some lyrics from a song that I wanted to give to you. It is me talking to you:

'When you think you cannot do this anymore, that is what my love is for.

When you're weak, I'll be strong.

When you let me go, I'll hang on.

When you need to cry, I'll be there to dry your eyes.

I'm gonna love you through it.

When you feel lost, scared to death,

like you can't take one more step, together we can do it.

I'm gonna love you through it.

When this road gets too long,

I'll be the rock you lean on. Together we can do it.

I'm gonna to love you through it.'

I love you, mom."

Evan: She would have the ability to find one or two words, or a lyric, that keyed in perfectly on what she was trying to express to you. In this case, she was trying to comfort Donna, trying to say, "It's okay. I'm with you."

14 – THE END IS NEAR

Jennifer: Nobody knows when his or her time is up. That is why it is so important to just live for each day. I was taught to fight, to never give up and that is a lesson I will take with me to my grave. I will find my happiness in my sunny surroundings, the gritty sand on my feet and the sun in my eyes and a future so bright I "gotta wear shades."

Starting the final decline

Evan: Even though Jennifer's death was a surprise to me when it came, she was big time in decline over her last few years.

Fibrosis, if you look it up in the dictionary, it's a string. The lung tissue becomes damaged, scarred if you will, and it becomes fibroid, or stringy in other words. Eventually, the lungs stop being functional. In Jennifer's case, by the time she died, her lung capacity was probably down to 25-28%.

Donna: It was hard for Jennifer to do things.

Evan: It was hard for her just to take a shower. Mark always had to carry her up the stairs.

Donna: She only said one thing to me one time when we were Skype-ing ... she says, "Mom, you just don't know how hard this is." I just pushed it away and changed the subject, because she told me that I could never be negative. I always have to be positive, so I could never say anything negative. I really never got a chance to talk to her about dying, or what her wishes were or stuff like that because I couldn't bring up negativity.

Evan: No. It was her wish, and we respected her too much. As much as it might have been healthy to have that type of discussion on occasion, she said specifically, "I ain't going there." Guess what? We never went there.

Donna: Jennifer did tell me once that she felt she would die of Cystic Fibrosis ... You know what? Maybe she wouldn't bring up those subjects because she knew that it would kill me.

Evan: How hurtful it would be.

Donna: She knew all of my buttons and what pushing each one can do.

Last six months

Evan: I'm almost ashamed to admit that I don't know what the last six months of her life was like. It hurts. I wanted more time. If I opened up my journal, you would see entries in there like, "I need to see Jennifer" or "I need to smell Jennifer," because I just loved her smell. If we were there or she were here, I would have seen her every day or every other day and maybe just for 10 minutes or maybe 10 hours, I don't know. But I would have known, day to day, what it took her to get through the day. Instead, I only know what she said on the phone, over Skype, and we usually didn't dwell on the negatives.

Where's religion?

Evan: Religion never played a huge role in me growing up or Donna growing up. I think I can speak for her. Extreme pride in our heritage, in my case over-the-top pride. To the point even now, 70-80 years later, I know I lost relatives in the Holocaust, and it still bothers me. The concept of the Holocaust is so overwhelming, and what the world lost because of that. It drives me insane sometimes.

We do observe the Jewish holidays to the best of our ability. We don't light candles every Friday night. We don't go to synagogue on Friday night or Saturday morning. Early on, when we had Jennifer, we talked about it, joining a temple, going to Sunday school, or Saturday school, becoming bar mitzvahed, all of that. Donna made the decision not to get involved to that degree, and I supported that decision. I didn't agree with it 100%, but I supported it.

Our priority was Jennifer – keeping her healthy. We used the weekends when she was young to let her recharge her batteries. Sleep 'til noon, whatever. Having another day where she would have to get up at 6:00 or 7:00 in the morning to do what we had to do, and then get her to school, religious school, and then be exposed to additional children. Donna made the decision, no way. I said, "Okay," and that was it.

Jennifer knew she was Jewish. I tried to explain in my own way what her heritage was, but we lived in a community that wasn't predominately Jewish, like the one Donna grew up in where she wasn't exposed to a lot of Jewish influences. I give Jennifer credit – she knew she was Jewish, and she would carry some of the traditions over to a certain degree, and some of the Yiddish words for example. She didn't totally close the door on who she was. I like to look at it as she opened up the door wider and brought it all together, to her credit.

One aspect of it ... I think Jennifer was uncomfortable to a certain degree with the stereotypical description of what a Jew is – aggressive, money hungry, pushy, that type of thing. The stereotype is total BS in my opinion, but that's what people do. They take a group of people – whether it's Jews or Muslims or Catholics or Mormons, whoever – they find and identify the isolated, abhorrent behaviors, and they try to make you think that everyone's like that, which is crazy, but that's what they do. That's what Hitler did.

Anyway, Jennifer wasn't comfortable with that image. Unfortunately, because I wasn't able to teach her about Judaism, she didn't have a good understanding of what it was to be a Jew. Because she was influenced by other things and people, it was easier for her to understand the Christian way of life, let's say. So, when Mark came along – he's not a heavily practicing religious person, but they celebrated Christmas and they did go to church. It was nondenominational, and what they wanted to do was bring different types of people together.

Over a period of a few years, I learned to accept where she was. Although she and I never talked about it, she knew exactly how I felt, and I knew how she felt. I respected her and she respected me. When it comes to faith, believe me, in the last four and a half years, I've had many times of reflection and discussions about faith and spirituality, looking for answers, looking for understanding.

Faith and spirituality

Evan: Jennifer was a complex person spiritually. Part Jew – did not give up her Judaism in any way – but she also encompassed certain segments of Christianity that she found comfort with. I applauded that. Didn't agree with it, but I respected it, and I applauded her decision to find something that made her comfortable.

Donna: If it was comforting to her, it was okay by us.

Evan: Maybe it was to our detriment. I don't know. I can see someone saying that we weren't strong enough on the religious or the spiritual side, and that's why she didn't encompass Judaism 100%. I can see that, but that wasn't us. Donna made the decision long ago, as far as religious training goes. In the Jewish religion community, there's weekend Saturday school, sometimes Sunday school ...

Donna: You said this already. Go on.

Fear of death?

Donna: I know that she talked to her friend, Melody, and she did tell Melody that she's afraid that if she dies, that she'll miss Mark so much. That's the only thing I know she said about fear of death.

Sense of afterlife

Evan: Jennifer believed in it. And, for me, it's something that I'm fighting in my own head right now, probably because of my journey. Before I started my journey, I would say, "Give me a break. Come on. You're gone, you're gone." I'd accept the fact you can't destroy energy but, as far as it being manifested in a traditional heaven/hell type of situation, no. Even to this day, if I'm honest with myself, it's really hard for me to believe in an afterlife.

But I understand now why people think that way. Before, I didn't. It's because it gives them comfort. It takes away some fear. It makes things less scary. I get all that. I didn't before I got sick. I do now. Now, that doesn't mean I accept it as truth for me, personally, but I understand.

Donna: With all the books that I've read on near-death experiences and with me personally being spoken to by Jennifer through a medium, I have to believe that I will see her. Jennifer died on December 5th and, on January 24th, I went to see a man named Thomas John. He picked me out of the audience. He told me that I lost a child – that she died too soon – and that her name was Jennifer. She's with Evan's parents, James and Bea, and she's also with Sophie, Jennifer's dog. There's no way on earth that this man would know all these things. It's not written down anywhere. He names Mark – he told me that Mark, her husband, was very good to her. I mean, he just said so many things that he couldn't have known.

He asked me if I knew that I was going to connect with her, and I said, "Yes, because I talk to her all day long and tell her she better come through." I mean, so many people ... there's a neurosurgeon – Eben Alexander – the least likely type of person to believe in something like this – he saw his biological sister after she had passed that he didn't even know. So, what is that all about? It just can't come out of nowhere. There has to be something. I mean, I'm hoping and wishing that I connect with Jennifer. I think I will.

Evan: I vividly remember one particular hug with Jennifer. She was at college and we were getting ready to leave and all of a sudden we hugged. We embraced each other as a father and daughter should. That was cool – two humans, father-daughter, in tight embrace – and I even remember how she smelled. All of that is what I would like to do again. And, like Donna, I believe that maybe I will.

Final breaths

Evan: We do not know what the last stages of Jennifer's life were like. I wish I did know. But, now that I'm in a somewhat similar place, I have some ideas. Oh, for just one deep, fresh breath ... What I hope is that it was as peaceful as possible, that the pain was minimal and, most important, that fear did not raise its ugly head to her. That's what I want. But we weren't there, so we don't know.

Donna: I don't know what happened, other than, I think, at around 5:00 in the morning Jennifer screamed to Mark she can't breathe. They called the ambulance, and in half an hour she was dead. I don't know what they determined was the official cause of death.

Evan: I have to assume ... I know, I think, just because of who I am and what I do, that she exploded. Her lungs exploded.

Donna: Like some cyst that popped.

Evan: That's what I meant. That she exploded.

Donna: If I had to describe the last stages of her life, I would say it was happy, sad, full of great friends, loving Florida, and being hopeful that she'd get a second chance.

Evan: I'm glad you said that. My answer was ... should have included that. I'm glad you did.

Last Communication

Evan: Jennifer died on December fifth. The day before – on December the fourth – I had texted her. I was recalling a year ago at that time, it was nice out here, it was warm. I don't remember the specifics, but I complained to her that I wasn't going to play golf this year, for whatever reason, like I did last year. Her answer was, "Oh well." Those were her last words to me. That's all I got, but I didn't delete it.

Donna: On the house phone, there are two messages that I kept.

Evan: When you go into voicemail it says, "You have two saved messages." If I push the wrong button by mistake and I hear her voice, it hurts.

Donna: I like to listen to them, because I need to hear her voice. The last one that she had sent was for my birthday, which is the 30th of January.

Evan: The day after Jennifer's.

Donna: Yes, her birthday is the 29th, so she sang a song – "happy birthday, it's my birthday, too." After she passed, I still played it on my birthday, just to think that she was wishing me a happy birthday.

15 – THERE ARE NO ALLIGATORS IN HEAVEN!

Jennifer: Just being there and not saying anything is some-times needed. You saved me from the alligators, and I wish I could save you from this. Whatever way I can, I will.

Announcement of death

Evan: The phone rang approximately 8:00 in the morn-ing, on Saturday.

Donna: I was getting ready to go work out.

Evan: Right, and I was still in bed.

Donna: Evan was in bed. I got the phone call, and I see, it's Jennifer. I got very excited, because Jennifer didn't get up that early.

Evan: She thought it was the transplant.

Donna: She's calling to tell me, because we had to get on a plane ... They made arrangements for us, and we were going to stay in a certain ... There were all kind of arrangements ...

Evan: It was all set, it was Southwest Airlines and every-thing.

Donna: "Hello." It's my son-in-law. "I'm sorry to tell you, Jennifer passed away this morning." I started screaming. Michael started shaking. He knew what it was. After the phone call, and I immediately made arrangements to get a flight out to Florida, and we left that afternoon.

Only regret

Evan: The only regret I have is time. I regret that I didn't spend more time with Jennifer, especially at the end. We did not see her very often over those last four, five years – after she and Mark moved to Florida.

Donna: We tried to go twice a year. With the cost of it and, when she started on oxygen, we couldn't stay at her house, because they were sleeping in separate bedrooms, and there was no place for us.

Evan: We were her parents. If that meant just sitting in her house because she couldn't do anything, I didn't give a shit. I could care less. Go to the beach? Who cares? Go to the pool? Who cares? Not having more time with Jennifer is the only regret I have.

Saying goodbye ...

Donna: If I had a chance to talk to Jennifer again, there is nothing that I would say to her that she hadn't heard before. Because I always told her that I was so proud of her, that she grew up such a wonderful person, and that she was my hero.

When I do see her, what I would want to say to her that I wasn't able to say to her when she was alive? Well, as strange as it may sound, the thing I would want to say is "goodbye" because I never got to say goodbye to her. And that's the only thing I regret – I never got to say goodbye.

Evan: Same for me. Didn't have a chance to say goodbye to my father. Didn't have a chance to say goodbye to Jennifer. That's why I developed my silly little good-bye tour with my close friends and family – it gives me a chance to say goodbye.

Donna: In fact, her girlfriend told me that, even though Jennifer was already deceased when the friend got to the hospital. "I held her hand." I'm jealous that she got to hold her hand and I didn't.

Friendship with Melody

Evan: When Jennifer lived in Florida, she also developed a relationship with a woman in Jacksonville that she met online. They both had CF, were approximately the same age, they were at approximately the same stage, and they became very close.

Donna: Melody.

Evan: Melody, right.

Evan: They helped each other although, from what Melody told us, Jennifer helped her more than she helped Jennifer, but they always wanted to see each other and they couldn't. So, they never met. But Melody showed up at the funeral, unbelievable. She said she had to be there.

Memorial service

Evan: We were in Tampa Airport by 3:00, 4:00 that afternoon. The people on the airline, American I think, they were wonderful. Mark came to pick us up.

Donna: He came with his friend to pick us up. I said, "Do you want us to stay in a hotel?" "Oh, no. You're staying here." I said, "Okay."

Evan: That was on a Saturday. We went with Mark, and his brothers, and his parents, to the funeral home. Donna and I deferred everything to Mark.

Donna: We had no say so.

Evan: I didn't want to have say so, it wasn't my place. I'm talking about me.

Donna: I didn't want to say so, but the way it was done was excruciating.

Evan: That's different. I don't think Mark planned that. It was an open casket ...

Donna: ... for four hours?

Evan: ... for four hours.

Brief gathering

Donna: There was no burial. She was going to be cremated,

Evan: Afterwards, we went back to their friend's house.

Donna: Her best friend had everyone back with food and stuff. Everyone was just beautiful. Her friends, his family, they were just wonderful.

Evan: We have very close friends that live in Florida, on the east side, Delray Beach, right next to Boca. They said, "You're coming home with us." We didn't really talk about it, we just said, "Okay," which was the right decision.

Donna: We only had a one-way ticket there, because we didn't know what was going to happen. Jennifer died on a Saturday, her thing was on Wednesday, we left Thursday with our friends.

Evan: It was the right thing to do, because for Donna and me to come back here at that time would have been not good. We stayed with Michael and Karen, I don't know, five days maybe?

Donna: Yeah, and we were busy every day ...

Evan: Our friend, Michael, said to me, "What do you want to do? I'll do whatever you want to do." Like I am with everything, I boil it down to its most simple thing, and I said, "My choice is I can sit at your pool and cry, or let's go play golf."

So, we played golf. They belong to a private place. People would give their left arm to live like they do. We go to the pro shop, and he set me up with a set of clubs, and I just played in my gym shoes, and I had on a pair of shorts. There was one hole, I ended up in the sand right near the green. I chipped it out, and it rolled right into the hole. I went, "Thanks, Jennifer."

From that day on, every single time I played, any time I did something that I thought was out of the ordinary, I'd say, "There we go ..."

Melody saw a light

Donna: Jennifer's friend Melody told us that one night, before she knew that Jennifer had died, she noticed that a light outside of her house was shining very brightly. Melody later made the connection that it was right about the time that Jennifer passed away.

There are no alligators in heaven!

Evan: When Jennifer was little, we were in the townhouse, so she had to be five, six years old. She would come in to our bedroom, I'm going to say Sunday mornings, and of course that was like ... you know, she'd stand there and just look at you. I'd open one eye, peek out, and there she was. She'd shake her body like that, and she said, "Daddy, the alligators." I would grab her, and I'd lift her up onto the bed, and I would hug her and say, "I saved you from the alligators." We would laugh. We'd wrestle and we'd laugh. We did it all the time.

Then doing the routine CF things became part of saving her from the alligators. Donna would say, "Come on, let's go. We got to do blah, blah, blah," and then we went on our day. Or, "Do the X-Y-Z, we got to get going here. Got to save you from the alligators." That went on for maybe a couple of years till she grew out of it, as she should. I never forgot.

At her wedding ... as a parent of the bride, I stood up to say a few words about Jennifer. I recapped her life, or whatever, and I ended by saying to Mark, "It's your turn. Now you have to save her from the alligators."

And, finally, here's what I said at Jennifer's funeral ... No one fought harder, with more courage against the unrelenting savagery of Cystic Fibrosis. Jennifer's intelligence, dignity, and faith, provide a guide for all to fight each day to stay alive. Jennifer, our beautiful Jennifer, there will not be a day that goes by without you in our thoughts. You are now safe. You are now comfortable. Your pain and fears are all gone now. Don't forget, beautiful Jennifer, there are no alligators in heaven.

Jennifer Hale
January 29, 1972 – December 5, 2015

16 – REFLECTIONS

Jennifer: Through this journey I have had family and friends supporting me every step of the way and I cannot thank them enough.

Reflections by Jennifer's friends & colleagues

Sweet Jennifer, you faced an entire lifetime of physical struggles with such grace, optimism, and with a beautiful smile. You always inspired me. You have your mother's laugh and your father's walk, and a sweetness that was all your own. I will never forget you for so many reasons. — *Ginger* (Friend)

From Jennifer, I learned what it meant to be a strong person ... She took everything in stride. She would always find the silver-lining in everything she did. She was one of the most positive people I ever knew, which amazed me every time I talked to her. She never wanted you to feel bad for her. She knew she had a debilitating disease, but fought it hard every single day of her life. She never wanted it to control her, and it didn't. Up until the end, she still mustered the energy to work out (even with her air canister). She was truly an amazing person. I miss her every day, but her strength stays with me. — *Sandi* (Friend)

The night I met Jennifer Codell was a night I will remember for the rest of my life. She was beautiful and had an amazing smile. A bright smile that no one with CF would ever have. We talked about CF ... We also talked about college and how college helped her give her independence and responsibility of going away to school, meeting new friends, and not having mom and dad tell us when we should be doing our medication. She encouraged me to go away to school and not to worry about CF. It was part of her life but never stopped her from enjoying life. She said CF takes a backseat to enjoying life and college was a big step but an important step in achieving goals and dreams.
— *Jeff (Friend)*

Jennifer was a remarkable young lady. She had strength and endurance that were beyond my comprehension.
— ***Anne*** *(Friend)*

We loved Jennifer - she served on our board and was the consummate optimist. Her column articles were always uplifting and kind. We will miss her sorely. We really were all so shocked and saddened by her sudden passing. — ***Jeanie Hanley*** *MD, President, U.S. Adult Cystic Fibrosis Association, Inc., publishers of CF Roundtable*

Jennifer was a do-good kind of person, always succeeded in all avenues, a great story teller/writer for sure. (That's why it was no surprise when she started to blog later in life) ... and she made light of a heavy situation. She didn't wear her disease on the outside until she was an adult so many didn't know of it or at least not the severity of it and she was ok with that, but it meant she suffered a lot in silence. I was so proud to see as an adult she came out more, speaking and sharing to help others in their struggle. She was a real-life super hero for sure!

Our rekindled friendship allowed me to see her shine, to be a role model, a bride, a spiritual person, and someone who forgave. She didn't allow CF to define her. — **Lisa** *(Friend)*

One thing that stands out about Jen: She really cared about her friends. She was always a good listener and sounding board and had great insight for me if I had a problem. She had great emotional intelligence and depth and such

Adjectives used to describe Jennifer Hale by her friends and colleagues

a huge capacity to love everyone. What I took away from knowing her: Make time for your loved ones, for you know not what tomorrow may bring. I wish I could have had one more day with her ... but then I would just want one more. — **Julie** *(Friend)*

A good friend can change your life. — **Norm** *(Friend)*

Jennifer is an incredible human being. She is always eager and willing to speak with anyone about Cystic Fibrosis and what her daily life is like. She is also a wonderful advocate for the Cystic Fibrosis Foundation as she has consistently kept up with educating herself on our pipeline, directing people to the Foundation if they have questions and has raised thousands of dollars for vital CF research as a Great Strides Team leader. Although she has had some recent medical setbacks, I have never met anyone more determined to "keep going" – whether that be in her treatments, fundraising, or life in general.

— **Liz Burke**, *Greater Illinois Chapter, CF Foundation*

When I met Jennifer, it was as if we were both searching for the same friend and knew when we had found her. As someone once told me, good friends are not made. They are found ... Jennifer was the friend missing from my life.

She brought out the best in me because she saw the best in me. She made time to listen to my trivial problems because she knew they were not trivial to me. She showed me how to live life even though life isn't easy. Jennifer's unfailing faith in God and ability to laugh at the absurd are gifts that I will carry with me and share with others. You can endure anything if you have hope that things will get better.

I have struggled to understand why our time together was so short. We talked about all the great memories we would create with one another. We would paddle board. She would take my step aerobics class. We would vacation together. Spend the holidays together. I realize now we were creating memories - at her kitchen table, in her living room, simply sitting across a table from one another.

I prepared a summary of what I learned from her in what I call the *Tao of Jennifer* ... — **Kate** (*Friend*)

The Tao of Jennifer

1. *God is always on your side.*
2. *Be patient. The best is yet to come.*
3. *Life isn't fair, which is good, because we have more good in our lives than we actually deserve.*
4. *Take stock in your abundant blessings.*
5. *Remember to say thank you.*
6. *Worrying about the future is normal, but it's a waste of good time.*
7. *Laugh loudly.*
8. *Cry with your friends.*
9. *It's not about how many times you get knocked down. It's getting up that matters.*
10. *In order to be brave, you must know that something is scary.*
11. *Live every day the best you can, knowing that "your best" is not the same every day.*
12. *Give yourself permission to catch your breath.*
13. *The secret to being happy is not a short O. It's B positive.*

EPILOGUE

by Evan Michael Codell *(December 12, 2016)*

When I think of life with Jennifer, I recall many happy times. There were so many because we tried to make each moment happy. Of course, we couldn't, but we made every effort to make whatever we were doing a happy moment. Some stood out more than others. But really any time she laughed was a happy moment. It could be something as simple as a silly smile or it could be much more complex. She had a wonderful laugh, much like Donna's, and it was infectious. It didn't take much to get a happy moment out of the three of us because we were just happy people. Happy and grateful, so we all knew how important each happy moment was and somehow, someway, we should embrace the moment as best we could.

Unfortunately, I also think about sad times. There were many of those, too. The news from the doctor or nurses always wasn't positive. They wanted to do a new test, or they wanted to do this or they wanted to do that. Well, it's all about attitude, and we tried to instill in Jennifer the adult approach, where you say, "okay, one more thing." But still the constant testing was sad. It was also sad when we occasionally had to say "no" because something could be detrimental to her health. It could have been something like a sleepover, and we'd have to explain why not her. It hurt as a parent to have to explain why certain things could not be done. But, like I've said before, it's the same thing as having to brush your teeth – you just do it.

I only remember one time where Jennifer basically said, "Why me?" We were at Children's Memorial, and they wanted to do a test in the nasal cavity where they would have to insert a long Q-tip into the nasal cavity to extract fluid. Not a pleasant idea ... She looked at me and, I can see her now, she said, "Dad, this isn't fair. This is not fair. Why do I have to do this? Why was I picked as the one to carry all this?" And I remember answering, "Because whoever does the picking felt you were strong enough and even wise enough to work your way through the challenges that you would face." And she did – she tried so hard and so long to clean herself out so she could take one more deep fresh breath, like I'm trying to right now. In the end, she couldn't, and it was a hard struggle.

Along the way, Jennifer always insisted on being told the truth. Even when she was little, she always wanted to know the truth. "Daddy, tell me the truth. Daddy, tell me the truth." This created a problem because you surely don't want to hurt anyone, so telling her the truth had to be tempered. But in general we found that the truth, as the old saying goes, shall set you free. A lot of families don't realize how strong, how resilient our kids are.

As Jennifer's father, all along I wanted to be physically strong and physically active so that she could take strength from me. We set a tone in our house that physical fitness was what we do. Who we are. I was driven to keep her as strong as possible so, when the time ultimately came for a fix, she'd be physically strong – her body would be in good shape to accept what it was about to go through. As it turns out, she was approved for a lung transplant – a remarkable achievement. Unfortunately, we ran out of time.

Time is precious, and that is my only regret. Despite all the early mornings that I would have breakfast with Jennifer before I went to work – even when she was in the hospital. (She'd have three pieces of toast with cinnamon and butter.) In the end, I just didn't give her enough time.

When you consider our family, all three of us have our rough edges, all three of us have made mistakes, all three of us made decisions that we would like to take back. But that's part of being alive. We basically did the best we knew how to do under the circumstances that were stacked against us. And we came out, I guess, okay, except for one important ingredient: We lost her.

Looking back on all this, there is only one time where I felt like I was truly brought to my knees. Only one time for me, and it's very simple: December the 5th, 2015 – the day Jennifer died ...

Losing a child ... it's not supposed to be. This is abnormal. This is an aberration. This isn't what life is. And people are just ... they don't know what to say. I think, for whatever reason, people are afraid, and they don't know what to say, so they say the silliest things, and they think that what they're saying is going to make you feel better. But nothing they say will change the loss of your child.

The open wound will never be closed or healed or even dealt with. Maybe time will smooth out the rough edges. I don't know. Visitations, words, they are of no help to me. No one, not even the greatest wordsmith could offer a word, a phrase, that would change anything or make me feel better. Only a warm smile, a tender hug, and time can help. I mean that with Jennifer, and I surely mean that for me. I'm almost like a crazy man these days trying to get the word out to other people about how to treat people that are on my journey.

I refer to it as the journey and, until you take that first step on the journey, you can't know what it's like. I told someone the other day who didn't understand, "When you're confronted with a friend or family that is on the journey, instead of saying, 'How are you today?' or whatever, ask your friend or whoever this question: 'Who do you want me to be for you today?' and then shut up and let them tell you, and then do what they tell you. That's the best you can do." Sometimes they may want a hug from you, sometimes they may want you to listen to them rant for a while, or sometimes they may just want your silence.

I've come a long way and, the longer I've been on my journey, the more I understand how people who are terminally ill can find comfort in their faith, because faith answers questions that otherwise can't be answered. It gives people like Jennifer, and like me, some comfort to believe that there may be something. I don't know. When Jennifer passed away, we used to hear things like, "She's in a better place," and I would think, "Are you out of your mind?" Now I understand. Back then, even a year ago, I didn't get it. I get it now.

Through it all, Donna and I have been a team – we lived it 50/50 – and I have said already that there was no pre-plan on our part but it turned out that, whenever Jennifer was well, I was great and Donna was a mess. And it reversed when Jennifer wasn't doing well – I was the mess and Donna was the strength. Why? I don't know.

I'd be a fool to deny that the weight of Donna's psychological condition over the years was heavy. But what do you do? I couldn't leave them – you don't do that to people. She wasn't doing it on purpose. She wasn't doing it to get back at me. We never blamed each other. We just wanted to be good people, good parents. To be honest, watching Donna navigate all that she had to go through and still come out on top, if you will – it's amazing.

I want Donna to know how proud I have been to walk this walk with her. Most people that I've encountered don't have the depth of her strength. While we made mistakes along the way, the mistakes were made for all the right reasons. So, when I think about words for Donna, it's basically to keep doing what you've been doing for 43 years and that will carry you through.

And my words of advice for a young couple who find themselves in the same situation that Donna and I found ourselves back in 1974, when Jennifer was first diagnosed: *Just hold on to each other. Hold on to each other and make each other the most important people in your lives. It's the circle of the mother and the father and the child. They're the only ones that really count now – your obligation is only to each other and to the child, and you should always do what you think is the right thing to do.*

Lastly, know that you're not by yourself, and you shouldn't be by yourself. There's someone there who will bend over and pull you up. And you know what? You should let them pull you up. Once you're standing up straight, then you'll look around and begin to see things differently.

Evan Michael Codell
May 25, 1945 – December 14, 2016

APPENDIX

Jennifer Hale was a regular contributor to the *CF Roundtable: A Newsletter for Adults with Cystic Fibrosis* from Spring 2011 through Autumn 2015. The articles that she wrote during this period are reprinted here in full to create a complete record of Jennifer's thoughts, feelings, fears, inspirations, and insights. They are reprinted by permission of USACFA Inc., the publishers of *CF Roundtable.* More information on *CF Roundtable* is available at: http://www.cfroundtable.com/.

READER

Articles by

Jennifer Hale

1972–2015

Column: "Coughing with a Smile"

The articles included in this special *CF Roundtable Reader* were originally published in *CF Roundtable,* with volume and issue numbers indicated in the table of contents on the previous page.

They are reprinted here by permission of the US Adult CF Assn, Inc. (USACFA), the publishers *of CF Roundtable.*

Meet the
the New Director

Jennifer Hale

JENNIFER HALE

SUMMER 2012

Hello CF *Roundtable* readers. I am Jennifer Hale. I hope you have been enjoying my column "Coughing With A Smile". I am proud and honored to say I am now one of the new directors of USACFA! A little background about me: I was diagnosed with CF at the age of two and I am proud to say I am now 40 with CF and CFRD. I spent most of my life in the suburbs of Chicago and now live in sunny Florida with my wonderful husband to whom I have been married for 15 years. We love the weather and all the available outdoor activities here in Florida. I went to college at Eastern Illinois University and went on to work full time for a few years until having to take an early medical retirement. Now my days are filled with caring for myself, my health and my husband. I enjoy being active and love the beach. My FEV$_1$ has decreased, but I have just modified my lifestyle and activity to adjust. The latest adjustment for me has been my portable oxygen tank that I use while exercising in the local gym. Nothing will stop me. Keep on keeping on! I look forward to hearing from the readers of CF *Roundtable* and I hope to write inspiring, motivating and funny articles. Thank you. ▲

Coughing with a Smile

I did not ask for this
CF Roundtable, Spring 2011

I did not ask to be consumed with mucus that is sticky and looks and feels like wet cement.

I was born a bouncy, vibrant, cuddly baby girl. Perfect in every way with a future so bright, like the song goes, "you gotta wear shades." But the bright future was slowly presenting a huge black dot on the horizon. At the age of 2, I was diagnosed with Cystic Fibrosis (CF), a genetic killer of a disease, which is slow and merciless in its quest to consume and kill me. I was also born a fighter with a laugh that echoes throughout the heavens above and a positive attitude that does succumb to the dark side now and then.

I did not ask for this disease that is slowly killing me and robbing me of the very breath that I need to sustain my life. I did not ask to be consumed with mucus that is

sticky and looks and feels like wet cement. Its very existence inside me is hardening me up from the inside, like
clay hardens into statue. But this "clay-like" substance is
not molding a beautiful statue that someday may memori-
alize a great human being, a symbol of freedom or a mon-
ument. This substance is suffocating me and slowly robbing me of my existence on this earth.

I did not ask for CF, but I will not go down without a
fight. I ask myself, at times, do I have the fight still in me?
Like an amateur boxer going 15 excruciating rounds
against the World Champ, can l answer the bell one more
time? What choice do I have? This is my lot in life, but l
did not ask for this. Every sickness is a set-back in lung
function. How many times can you hit the reset button
and have it reset the baseline lung function I need to
maintain? I strive to maintain a baseline lung function
that can easily plummet due to one tiny virus.

I did not ask for this, but I will do what I can to stave
off this dreadful disease. I will look to the ocean for my
strength and look to my husband for the love and courage
to keep fighting. I was taught to fight, to never give up
and that is a lesson I will take with me to my grave. But
after each round I am so beaten up. I wonder how many
times l can answer the bell that says the next round is
ready to begin. Ah, the sweet sound of beginning again.
Beginning again after each sickness that sets me back so
far I wonder if I can even see the end of the road.

I did not ask for this lung disease that offers an average
life expectancy of 37 years and soon I will be 39! I did not
ask for the because, when you can't breathe, it sure makes
it difficult to exist and live life. As they say, if you do not
have your health, you do not have much. I did not ask for

this, but who would? So, I will keep on keeping on and judge myself not on what I can't do but what I can do. I will find my happiness in my sunny surroundings, the gritty sand on my feet, and the sun in my eyes and a future so bright I "gotta wear shades."

Who I am
CF Roundtable – Autumn 2011

Hello! I am honored to be writing for CF Roundtable and I look forward to getting to know our readers. Here is a brief introduction of who I am, and then we can get to the topic at hand: "CF, It's Not Just for Children." I am 39 years old and was diagnosed at age two. I had lung issues that were thought to be allergies, but a sweat test told my parents otherwise. They were told that I had Cystic Fibrosis (CF) and the prognosis was not good. They were told to not expect their daughter to attend high school. That was in October 1974.

I am happy to say that October did not have to always be a dark reminder of CF. October was the month I married my wonderful husband! We now are able to replace a dark moment of a terminal diagnosis with the moment of a blessed marriage.

I got through high school and college, all at a standard pace, and dealt with the ups and downs of hospitalizations and sicknesses with a smile on my face. I had very supportive parents and still do to this day! As I have gotten older, CF has presented itself with a lot more complications in terms of CFRD, decreasing lung function, bowel issues, and whatever else that I can blame on CF, right?! HA! HA!

My daily regimen is full of nebulized drugs (three times-a-day), flutter/ vest, enzymes, insulin, blood glucose checks, exercise, lots of sleep and good nutrition. I was in the "rat race" out in the corporate world but could not stay healthy and finally came to terms that a disability retirement would be the right choice for me. I am "retired" and living in Florida. Wait, I am only 39, not 79 - LOL! I am enjoying Florida and just looking out at the beach and the open water really speaks to my soul.

I named my column "Coughing with A Smile" because I always try to look at the bright side of the situation. Also, as many people with CF experience in their own lives, a CF cough is distinctive and my husband always knows where I am when we are out in public. He follows my cough; it is his yellow brick road to me! Therefore, "Coughing with A Smile" seemed to be an appropriate name for my column.

Now, for the topic at hand. "CF, It's Not Just for Children." I love this topic!! The reason it strikes such a chord with me is that it is very hard for people to realize and comprehend the seriousness of living and breathing with adult CF. If I can count how many times I have been told, "You do not look like anything is wrong with you," I could have retired to Florida a long time ago! On a positive note, I am happy that this is a topic of discussion to begin with in the CF community. To be an adult with a "terminal" disease and see all the progress that has been made since I was diagnosed has been nothing short of amazing. Since CF is an orphan disease, I am so grateful for the advances that have come throughout the years in terms of the drugs, medical care and research. Living with CF as an adult now presents a lot of different obstacles.

Being an adult with CF has been very different from how things were when I was a child. As a child I was much more resilient in terms of my CF. My hospital stays were a chance to see my favorite nurses and to decorate my IV pole. As an adult I like to stay far away from the hospital, opting for home health care instead and explaining to people that the undecorated wrap around my arm is protecting my IV PICC line.

Being an adult means having to rely more on yourself to get through all the meds, therapies, tune-ups etc. It is hard to be your own cheerleader and motivator all the time! Lucky for me, my husband is a huge help and my parents still are in my corner!

When I was a young adult, my life was all about school and how I could get through college while being around people who might be sick in the classrooms. I had to maintain a social life and still be compliant with my care. I was able to stay compliant and get through college in only four years! At the same time, I did not do as many nebs as I do now. I did not have CFRD and my lung function was a lot higher than it is now. I am thankful I had increased lung function while getting through school and I was able to enjoy college life.

As an adult going into the corporate world, I had more control about avoiding "sick" people, or so I thought. I once again found it hard to stay away from people who had colds since everyone went to work sick and still does. It is the society we live in that, unfortunately, dictates there is no rest for the weary. I found that my own health was declining and I was not able to work in the "rat race." That is when I decided I needed to get on disability. What a hard decision that was to accept.

In your early 30s you are either working or working to have a family, and I was now doing neither! Disability was hard to accept, which is a whole other topic of discussion! Now my "JOB" is me and taking care of myself so I can stay as healthy as possible. The problem is that I cannot fire myself! I have to keep going and doing all the meds and therapies. My advancement is not promotions, raises, or a different job description. My promotion is being able to get through the night without sleeping on five pillows, getting out to the gym on a regular basis, ordering meds and supplies and doing all my therapies and medications on schedule.

Being an adult is also realizing what costs are associated with having CF. Whoa! Do the bills add up or what? Dealing with insurance companies is as frustrating as a bad itch on your back that you cannot reach. Now, not only am I an adult dealing with a terminal disease but also handling all the paperwork, insurance companies, doctor appointments and proper management of therapies and medications, too. I can go on and on; wait, maybe this is a JOB. I am the CEO of me!

Having CF as an adult means you also have to deal with the decision to have children or not. That was a big decision for me and to think I will never be called mommy, sometimes really pulls at my heart strings. My husband and I decided my health was too important and high maintenance, and to have a child would be too hard for us. That was our decision for us and what was right for our lives.

Now, it is just me and CF which is kind of like a baby. It does require lots of care, daily feedings and tons of attention! CF is not just for kids, and being an adult with CF presents a new set of complications and emotions. I sometimes wish the sympathy and empathy a child receives for dealing with a disease that is so horrendous would carry on into the adult life of someone with CF. The people who meet me cannot "see" the disease and people just do not always have that same compassion for an adult with a "hidden" disease that they would have with a child. But there are people I meet who do "get it," and that makes up for the trials and tribulations of dealing with CF as an adult. I am glad we can talk about CF adults and I am happy to have these "adult" problems to deal with in my life. CF is challenging and a rough road to walk. To have that chance to become an adult with CF is a wonderful opportunity. Don't take a day for granted and, as I always say, "Keep up the good fight; it is worth it!"

Until next time, my friends!

My special dog ...
CF Roundtable – Winter 2012

Sophie made me laugh, and laughing in turn made me cough, which was good therapy to get all my mucus out.

Well, hello again readers! I hope your holidays were full of blessings and good health! The topic at hand for this issue is: "Our Pets and How They Affect Our Lives." This is a topic that at one time I would not have been able to relate to, but I was blessed with experiencing what a pet can add to one's life – all the positives and all the negatives.

I grew up deathly afraid of dogs. It was so bad that when I went trick or treating with my cousin, he would have to get the candy for me if we heard a dog bark after we rang the doorbell. I would stand several feet away and wave as my cousin explained that I was scared of dogs, but I would like some candy. I think this fright came from the fact that when I was younger a dog chased me, climbed down my back and ran his paws with, what I thought were claws, down my hair. I ran to a tree and hugged it so hard, as this beast clawed down my back. I was scarred, and from that day forward I never got near dogs and was just so scared.

My mom and dad did not force me to get over this fear so my childhood was not filled with a Fido. I went as far as to have a fish and that did not last very long either.

Fast forward to an adult, married and living in the sub-urbs, and we get a call from my brother-in-law in Georgia asking if we would like a stray dog that he found. He said she was sweet, but he just could not keep her since he already had two dogs of his own. When my husband asked me if we could get this dog, the flashbacks of claws down my back entered my mind. You would think I was at-tacked by Cujo (and I was not), but in my mind every dog was Cujo. So, I said, "Why not? Let's do it! I need to get over this fear."

So, we packed up the car and drove to Kentucky to meet my brother-in-law and to pick up our new dog. Let me tell you this was not a lap dog. It was a 75 pound, black and white, Australian shepherd mix. What had I gotten myself into!?

We decided to name the dog Sophie. We started with Oreo 'cause she was black and white, but somehow in the little motel room the name Sophie emerged. For us,

Sophie was born into our lives, in a small Louisville, Kentucky motel, during Derby days in April of 2000.

When we got home we were completely unprepared to have a dog. We had no toys, no cage and just a big pillow bed for our untrained dog. Every time we would open the door to go outside she would run past us and down the street. She was gone before we could say sit. She loved people so she would stop along the way to visit with them. That gave us enough time to get in the car and down the street to pick up our runaway. She had some accidents in the house and for me, who is a neat freak, I was not digging that! I was VERY upset and told my husband that I just can't live with this dog. It is too much for me to handle. We decided to give it two weeks, at least, and get her some training.

The trainer came to the house, which was nice, and in no time had her sitting, lying down, walking by our sides, and recognizing her name. Slowly, Sophie came around, and so did I.

Sophie became my little baby. I can't tell you how many times my husband would hear me say, "Look at the little baby." I would even wrap scarves around her head and then laugh at her cause she looked like an old lady from a bad cartoon. She made me laugh, and laughing in turn made me cough, which was good therapy to get all my mucus out.

We came to realize, pretty soon after we had her, that she had a tremendously snotty nose. I mean snot would go flying all over the place from her nose. And it was yellowish/brown and I was thinking, "Does she have Cystic Fibrosis?" It was very appropriate for our dog to have a "snot" nose and lots of mucus production. I mean she really fit into the family! We were both now filled with mucus, only I had to wipe her nose and she could not do the same for me! LOL!

Sophie loved her walks. You could not say the word "walk" unless you were going to take her out for a walk. She knew the word and the tail started wagging and she was fired up to go for her walk. She would also run to the door and it was usually a chore to get the leash on her for her walks. We realized later in her life to not ask her if she wanted to go for a walk but to just put the leash on when she least expected it and then we would not have to deal with her convulsions of excitement. Sophie got me out-and-about for a walk and that was great exercise for my lungs. I thank her for all the exercise she provided for me.

Our beloved dog developed what the doctor thought was cancer, only seven short years after we had her. She was so good about her medicine. This is ironic since I am, too, about mine. See, she fits in just perfect for us! We would call to her and say, "It's time for your medicine," and she would come running. She would take her eye drops like a trooper. I like to believe she knew the word medicine and knew she needed to get her drops, but she also got a treat after each session. So, medicine to her could have meant, "Sophie, time for your treat." LOL! Whatever the reason, she came running and she was such a good and brave girl.

Towards the end of her short life with us, her health declined quickly. It was sad to see this food-motivated, walk-loving dog not want to budge from her pillow bed. Just to get her down the stairs to go to the doctor on the last day we had to tell her she was going for walk in order to get her down the stairs. So sad! I tear up just thinking of it now.

Putting Sophie down was one of the hardest things I have had to do in my life. She went peacefully and with those around her who loved her most. It was funny when we were in the room, she went up to my husband and nuzzled him and then she came over to me for a nuzzle. It was like she knew what was happening and she was saying goodbye. I like to think she was saying thank you for picking me and loving me. So, the dog who was never meant to be in my life enriched my life with a lot of love. She was the baby I would never have and taking care of her was a pleasure. May you rest in peace my special dog. Sophie came into our lives in April of 2000 and floated out of our lives on October 6, 2007.

Hey, at least the glass has something in it!
CF Roundtable – Spring 2012

Luckily, health and circumstances do change so that I can get better when I am ill and stronger when I am healthy.

Hello again readers! I hope this edition of CF Roundtable finds y'all embracing spring and the warmer weather that is approaching. So, the topic this time is "Am I A Pessimist or An Optimist?" Is the glass half empty or half full? As you can see from the title of this column; I think sometimes one has to just be glad there is any liquid in it at all. Life is not perfect and dealing with CF is anything but perfect.

According to Amy Grant, "Sometimes the greatest act of faith we can muster is just putting shoes on in the morning." When I read this quote, I could really relate to it because, sometimes for those dealing with CF, that is about all we have. I find that to be okay. Some days are going to be better than others. Growing up, I was taught to be a fighter, confront each battle with CF and keep myself as healthy as possible to win the CF war! I find in the forty years I have been battling CF, I take this optimism with me for each challenge in my life, whether it be CF-related or not.

Amy Grant also once said that, "Nothing stays the same, even if we want it to and, thankfully, especially when we don't." How true is this? When I am feeling bad I want that to pass quickly! Luckily, health and circumstances do change so that I can get better when I am ill and stronger when I am healthy. Hey, that sounds like an optimist! I told myself recently on the good days I should go for it and on the bad days I will just work through it. That has really helped me this past year or so.

My health took a grave turn in 2011 and I am still battling the residuals from that year. It is hard to always be optimistic when nothing is going your way and you are not feeling well, no matter how hard you are trying. CF is unpredictable and I find over the years I have had to adjust my sails. A Facebook friend of mine recently posted a quote that said, "The pessimist complains about the wind, the optimist expects the wind to change and the realist adjusts the sails." Anonymous. When I thought about this quote I felt it was very true. I do think about the worst possible scenario in a situation, but then I go right on adjusting my sails so I can deal with the different outcomes and stay positive that the light will shine at the end of the tunnel. I tend to approach all problems in my life like this, and I really feel it is because I have CF and had to deal with it from a young age.

I was diagnosed at the age of two and spent my fair share of time in the hospital for "tune ups" while missing out on school events and other events in my adult life. I find that in dealing with CF there are a lot of complications and different conditions that arise from having CF, whether it be CFRD, CF-related arthritis or gastrointestinal problems - just to name a few. I always have to weigh out possibilities and outcomes.

Unfortunately, when dealing with a chronic illness, bad things happen and I find my first thought is to prepare for the worst-case scenario but then to stay optimistic and fight all the way through – to keep adjusting the sails but to be aware that a storm can come in and blow me off course. Then I adjust the sails again and again!

I don't feel that because I review the worst-case scenario in a situation it means I am a pessimist. It is just how I process through a problem. I need to know all the outcomes, both the good and the bad. And I keep the bad outcome on the back burner but keep stirring the pot of the good outcomes. I feel this comes directly from living with CF. I always need to know what is the worst that can happen, what treatment would be needed and, then, what we are now going to do about it. I like to know my options, but I focus and put energy in the positive option or, more importantly, the option I can control. I practice very hard not crossing the bridge until I come to it! So, I feel I am an optimist and realist.

CF is part of me just like my brown eyes and my brown hair so I feel, of course, it is going to influence how

I deal with all situations in my life. Dealing with a chronic illness makes one grow up real fast because one is faced with challenges and decisions beyond her years. I feel this has enabled me to be thoughtful in my decision making and able to deal with each curve ball of life. Life is messy, with or without CF. As preacher Joel Osteen once said, "Troubles are inevitable, misery is optional." I opt to not be miserable; it is a waste of time and energy.

I do have to say that being my own cheerleader all the time is tough. I have wonderful support from my husband and family but, in the end, it is up to me! It is up to me to do all my treatments and do all I can to stay or get healthy. I can't tell you how many times I have thought, "I wish I could just take a pill!" Welcome Kalydeco into the picture! The pharmaceutical companies have come a long way in creating CF drugs and will continue to keep surprising us old timers with new and exciting treatments. Optimism is at the doorstep of new technology and this new science is going to enable people with CF to live longer and/or more productive lives. So, all in all, I think I am a realist with optimistic tendencies. Does pessimism rear its ugly head every once in a while? Of course; I am human, but I don't allow it to move to the front of the stove. It is on the back burner. It doesn't get the attention of a crafted meal on the front burner. I feel "circumstances can't dictate the way one lives; one must be stable in all the good and bad." This was said by Joyce Meyer, and being stable is what I strive for so that I can deal with all of it - "The Good, the Bad and the Ugly." Thanks Clint Eastwood!

Now I have to go drink my half glass of hot chocolate that is left. Thank you for the small things ...

Chatty chatty bang bang

CF Roundtable – Summer 2012

As I got older my health has declined, but my need to talk about my CF and to share ideas with other people with CF has increased. Hello readers of CF Roundtable. Hope this issue finds y'all doing and feeling well! The topic of this issue is about what you do while you are doing your treatments and what has worked. Well, for me, I simply watch TV or surf the net so writing a whole column on that was not going to take up much space – LOL! So, I thought I would write about CF forums and chat rooms and what I personally thought of them. Again, this is solely my opinion and I can always stand corrected. It's all good!

Growing up I did not want people to know I had CF I was luckily not real sick growing up and it was easy to avoid talking about CF, and I sure didn't look like I was sick. I still don't look like I have CF, but I am much worse as an adult health-wise. Funny you can never tell a book by its cover! I guess that is a whole other story. (Maybe I found my next column topic.) Anyhow, I was not into sharing my disease, promoting awareness about it or even talking to others with CF I did not go to the camps for CF patients. (Now I am dating myself! But that is good when you have CF, yeah 40!) I just did not want CF to be so much a part of my life, including being around or even talking to others who had it. I was not encouraged to do so by my parents and therefore I just did not find a need to have that connection and/or interaction.

When I was growing up, kids with CF did not fare as well as kids do now. There weren't all the wonderful medications and treatments like there are now and those with CF had a very uncertain future. We still have an uncertain future and I don't want to make it appear that having CF is a walk in the park, but the meds and therapies that are out in the year 2012 are a lot more advanced than in 1972.

I remember one time I was in the hospital for an exacerbation and a friend was doing a report and she chose to write about CF I was mortified and nervous that EVERYONE at school would know why I was in the hospital and then they would know that I had the disease she was reporting on for her school paper. I was very upset and, of course, when I got back to school no one even batted an eye. That was how secretive I was about my disease. I just did not want anyone to know. I suppose I just did not want to be perceived as different from everyone else. That was my choice on how to live my CF teen years but that all changed as I got older.

As I got older my health has declined, but my need to talk about my CF and make people aware of what I go through and to share ideas with other people with CF has increased. I found I enjoy talking to people about my CF experience and even more I enjoy talking with others who have CF or whose loved ones have CF Being 40 with CF, I have been around the block and to give hope to families whose small children have CF has been one of my greatest accomplishments. I now love talking about CF with people and sharing my story and experiences. It is a far cry from what I used to be like growing up, but this hope that I can share with others is sometimes just what that other person needs and that is a great feeling. This leads me to my opinion on forums and chat rooms for CF.

There are a couple of these chat rooms and forums to peruse in the CF community and I have actually met some really great people who I now talk to not only on the forum but also via phone. It has been great to share our stories, experiences and even laugh at some of the things CF people go through. It is really comforting to talk to someone who "gets it" and who has been through the same things I have, as well as things I haven't experienced. I get their honest opinion and first-hand experience of a medication, procedure, or therapy and that is priceless information. Yes, the doc can explain things thoroughly but the doc has not gone through it and "felt" it, so it is nice to ask my friends in the CF community what the real deal is.

Forums and chat rooms are GREAT to find some good information but I also feel one has to precede with caution. There are a lot of people on the boards with good ideas and some with really strange ones. Some people are really desperate in their CF walk and I personally feel desperate people sometimes make desperate choices. I feel you need to ask your doctor about any treatment or therapy before adding it to your routine.

There are some crazy ideas out there and people putting some crazy solutions in their nebs. But that is just one example. I also feel you can get wrapped up in someone's life a little too much which could add much stress to your own. So again, when I go on these forums I really try to listen a lot and proceed with caution. I remember one time I got so wrapped up in this one person's CF drama. A whole bunch of people on the forum were praying for this person, including myself. Come to find out the person was lying about having CF and it was this whole big story. I felt horrible. I mean I was praying for this person and looking at the updates daily and then come to find out the person was not afflicted with CF WOW! Like I said, red light, green light, YELLOW LIGHT!!!!!

On a better note, like I said before, I have met some great people through the forums and formed some real solid relationships. I have learned a lot from these forums and have asked my doc a lot of questions over the years just from information I read on the forums and chat rooms. Since we cannot be physically around someone with CF, having these places to go is a great alternative. It is a place where you can ask any question about what you're dealing with and you will get all kinds of responses. Some good, some bad and some that make you really think. It is a good resource to have at your fingertips and that is exactly how I use it - as a resource. I love that some people have emerged to become great friends and that is a bonus! The days of CF camps are over so now we have virtual camps and for the teens out there that is really a great thing. I know some people out there don't have a lot of support in their CF journey and these forums can provide support for them.

All in all, I am glad I am more open talking about my CF and it is nice to meet others from literally all over the world who are also dealing with the same issues I am on their CF journey. Hopefully we will all be able to share and support each other through the good times, bad times, and eventual cure for CF!

The numbers game
CF Roundtable – Autumn 2012

> *Change is always occurring and I notice I am always adjusting for each change.*

What is in a number? For those who suffer from disease a number could mean more medication, decline in health or time to make changes in your current regimen. A number can also bring hope. A number can indicate all is well in your body and you're on the right track. But there are times when the number is not where it is supposed to be and it is directly affecting how you feel and your prognosis. Numbers do not always tell the tale, but they are an indicator for me - a barometer to measure and compare my statistics of past tests. My body and how I "feel" tell me what my true number is. Am I feeling good mentally and physically? Am I able to get through my day with a smile on my face and feeling good? How can I feel "good" when my lung function is only 39%? How am I functioning? I suppose we all find out what our parameters are and adjust our sails to the wind of change. Change is a big word in the life of those who suffer from disease. Change is always occurring and I notice I am always adjusting for each change. Sometimes it is daily, sometimes it is weekly and even, sometimes, it can be hourly. But I can adjust with each change and it is a chance to turn it all around. Sometimes I cannot turn it around even if I try my hardest, but tomorrow is a new day.

Recently I had to undergo a Toupet Fundoplication or in layman's terms, an esophagus wrap. I had severe acid reflux and it was detected by my sputum culture and decline in lung function. My numbers were dropping and cultures; hence in my lungs! That is not supposed to happen and after doing several Acid Reflux tests, it was determined that I needed this surgery.

I was not crazy about getting it done because I never had surgery before, so this was all VERY new to me. What clinched it for me is when the surgeon said to me, "Is it fair to say that if a CF patient lives long enough they will need a lung transplant?" Through my tears, I said, "Yes, that in my opinion is correct." He then proceeded to explain that in order to preserve the lungs I have now and to protect my "new" lungs in the future, if and when I go down that road, then this surgery is necessary. For me, I thought to myself, I want to keep these old lungs for as long as possible. So, if I am going to give myself any fighting chance to do that, then this surgical procedure must be done. And if and when I get that miracle of new, bright pink lungs, then this surgery will allow those lungs to function at their utmost capacity. So, in the end it was a no brainer. Toupet Fundoplication, here we come! I say we because what happens to me happens to my husband, who is the light of my life.

On a side note, my husband stayed with me in the hospital all night long for two nights. He slept on something they called a bed but, instead, was that of a park bench. He pushed my pole down the hallways and gowned and latexed up when sitting in my room - ALL DAY LONG! Poor guy got a blister on his hands from wearing the latex gloves all day long. He is my Prince Charming! As I lay there in bed in pain, unable to care for myself and be an advocate for myself, my husband, my love, was my voice, my hands, my legs, my heart. He is truly my EVERY-THING.

The procedure is a tough one but manageable with pain pills! Got to love modern medicine! The procedure calls for the surgeon to wrap part of your stomach around the end of your esophagus so the acid cannot make it up the esophagus and seep into your lungs. The first two weeks were no picnic. The main problem is having Cystic Fibrosis while undergoing the surgery. I was unable to cough for two days and treatments were not the greatest. You see, it hurt so very bad to cough! It felt like my stomach was ripping apart. It hurt so bad, even with the pain meds, that it brought me to tears. Luckily, and thankfully, the pain that caused tears lasted only a few days; then it was just pain with no tears! I know that might not sound so much better but when you are going through it there is a big difference between pain that causes you to cry and pain that just causes you to wince. I will take wince. Rather I will take no pain at all! I am a baby! A 40-year-old, big, ol' baby. But, hey, I have been through a lot and continue to go through a lot so pass the Sippy cup! LOL! After two weeks, it got a lot better and at the three-week mark I was able to start eating solid foods. Weeks of shakes, jello, pudding, apple sauce and soup were getting old. I needed something that sticks to your ribs. Once starting food my stomach did not like it too much. I am still having diarrhea issues, gas, bloating and pain. Never fear. It is all getting better; it is just a very slow process. At the six-week mark, things are a ton better! I am eating pretty much anything I want; slow with small bites and pain is very minimal. The surgeon says it takes about three months before one can say they feel back to their good old self. November never looked so good!!!

My hopes are that I can recover from this with flying colors and I can get my 39% FEV1 lung function raised! It is scary to be that low and the demands that I put on myself to function like when I was FEV1 65% are just unrealistic. I am not that person anymore, but that does not mean I cannot be that person again or close to it! I am a firm believer in exercise and I hope to be able to start that soon, so I can work on this FEV1. I have to say that since I have not been able to exercise, I have been very diligent about doing an afternoon treatment and with using this plastic apparatus the surgical team gave me for my lungs. It is this plastic, hand held "thing" on which you take a deep breath and make a white cylinder rise. I find it really is great for working your lungs and taking deep breaths. It has helped during this time when exercise is non-existent and I plan to continue with this apparatus even when I have accomplished my goals.

Recovery is slow. Patience is needed and there are highs and lows. During my lows, I wrote a poem called TODAY that you can read in the Poetry Corner section of this CF Roundtable. I also have the poem posted in the BLOGS on the CF Roundtable website. I hope it helps you or someone you know as much as it helped me writing it out on paper.

Well, until next time readers. Hopefully I will be able to report that things are on the up and up!

What 'SUP?

CF Roundtable – Winter 2013

Stand Up Paddle-Boarding (SUP) is a great sport for all ages, genders, and disabilities.

Hello CF Roundtable readers! I hope the holidays are being kind to y'all and you are enjoying the season. I recently had the opportunity to be interviewed by a fellow person with CF here in Florida about Stand Up Paddle-Boarding. It is a port I recently was introduced to since moving from snowy Chicago to sunny Florida. I thought it would be fun to share with y'all the article we wrote together. The following paragraph was expertly written by my friend, Chris. I hope you find the following Q&A fun and interesting! Enjoy!

SUP (stand up paddle boarding) is the latest international fitness craze to take center stage. In all fairness, paddle boarding has been around since humans were using long sticks to push themselves around on floating logs; and while today's paddle boards may be more advanced, the same 'primitive' concept remains at the heart of the sport. SUP has really evolved in recent years and branched off to include recreational paddling, flat water racing, open water racing, surfing, and yoga. What makes SUP so appealing is the sport's ability to accommodate people with or without disabilities, at all skill levels, in a wide range of water conditions. People can stand, lie supine, kneel, and sit (on the board or on an inflatable seat attachment) as they paddle with their hand or use a single or double blade paddle. One can even add small sail attachments to get a little help from the wind. It's the versatility of SUP that allows it to compliment a variety of therapies that are beneficial to children/adults with Cystic Fibrosis. With such great potential as a therapeutic tool, there's no wondering why Cystic Fibrosis Surfing/SUP Experience Days are now sponsored throughout Florida and other parts of the United States. I recently had the opportunity to catch up with Jennifer Hale, a 40-year-old person who has CF and CF-related diabetes, and chat about how she benefits from SUP.

C: Aloha Jennifer.

JH: Hello readers out there! What 'SUP? How are you? LOL!

C: How did you get into SUP fitness?

JH: I am new to this sport and new to sunny Florida. I hail from the Windy City, so the only board I was familiar with was the one that rode on snow and down a mountain. Then I took a SUP class out on the Gulf of Mexico, when I first moved to Florida, and fell in love with the sport!

C: What do you find most appealing about SUP?

JH: When I moved to Florida I just had to get out on that water! Stand Up Paddle Boarding is a great sport for all ages, genders, and disabilities. SUP is a board that looks like a surf board and you can stand, kneel, or sit on it and paddle with an oar out into the water. The three aspects of it that I like the best are: ease of doing it, breathing salty air and the spiritual aspect of being out on the vast open space of the water. I really like to be out on the open water. It is really spiritual and peaceful for me.

C: Is there a particular reason why you prefer ocean conditions over freshwater conditions?

JH: Being out on the water you get all that natural hypertonic saline solution. Got to love medicine that comes naturally from Mother Nature. The salt in the water and, thus, in the air is really good for our lungs! I do not mind ocean or freshwater. What I do like is calm waters. When the water is calm, like out in the mangroves, it is easier to balance vs. when I am out in the gulf, the waves make it a different workout. So, it just depends on the kinds of conditions one prefers and the kind of workout one is looking for with the SUP.

C: I'm all for taking in free hypertonic saline treatments while enjoying a sunny day at the beach! Even though Florida waters are traditionally flat during the summer months, there is still small wave action in the Atlantic and Gulf waters. I would imagine launching your SUP board from the beach would be a challenge. How do you do it?

JH: You just have to go on the board like a surfboard, lying on your stomach, to get over the waves. Or you can just walk out into the water holding the board to your side and walking beside it. Once you get out past the waves you can lie on your stomach and paddle out to the more open water and then get your bearings to sit and/or stand up on the board. Launching from the gulf is more challenging than launching from a mangrove area because the gulf has waves vs. flat water. All in all, paddle boarding is very easy to do; and if you cannot stand on it then you can it. So, you are just floating around on this board and using your oar to paddle around. Once you get the hang of it you can stand up, which then will work your core muscles and use balancing techniques. What I like about this is if you are too tired it is easy to just sit and paddle on it like a canoe. I also like that you can hook some bungee cords to hold a little cooler for snacks and drinks. Having CFRD, it is important for me to have access to juice and with the depletion of salt from working out in the sun it is important to have those Gatorades handy. Even though I am out in the middle of the ocean I can still have my cooler with goodies attached to the board. Sitting or standing, it is a great workout and not too strenuous if you do not want it to be that way. You put into it what you want to get out. Paddle more or paddle less. Sit or stand. It is a fun workout.

C: With a vast majority of SUP boards longer than 9 feet, do you find SUPs challenging to transport on land and maneuver on water?

JH: I have not tried many lengths of boards on the water, so I'm not sure what the different lengths "feel" like out on the water. I can say carrying the boards is not as bad as it appears to be. They are lighter and have a space to put your fingers so you can carry the board. Being only 5'1", maneuvering a 9-foot or longer board is a workout in itself. The boards are not as heavy as they appear and there are shoulder straps and carts that you can purchase to transport your board. It's something to think about due to the size of the board relative to the person's size; and the condition of the person's health will factor in when deciding how to transport the board from land to sea.

C: What are your thoughts about using the paddle board to enjoy Florida's wildlife in and around our freshwater lakes, rivers, and natural springs?

JH: It is one of the best ways to see wildlife! True and funny story – I got my husband out on an SUP out in Ft. DeSoto and two manatees swam right up to his board. He did fall in and they swam away, but what a scene to witness! It's very cool what you can see on your SUP out in the open water. I have seen all kinds of fish, manatees, stingrays, and birds. It is so peaceful floating around the mangroves and seeing all this wildlife. If you have a waterproof camera, you can get some amazing pictures too! When you are out on the water you really feel like you are one with nature. The fish are right at your fingertips and it really is a cool scene to witness and be a part of.

C: I recently heard about the increasing popularity of using the SUP as a platform for yoga exercises. This is especially interesting to those in the CF community who already practice restorative yoga or one of the many other forms of yoga.

JH: Yoga is all about breathing and balance. I have not tried yoga on a SUP, but I would imagine it could be a good experience. You can put your board on dry land, shallow water or deep water depending on your yoga skill level. Balancing on the board coupled with yoga techniques would prove to be a really high powered yoga session! Yoga is also about mind, body, and spirit and what better way to incorporate all of that than out on the open waters with the wildlife and elements surrounding you!

C: Any words of encouragement you wish to share with the CF community?

JH: If you have an opportunity to try SUPing I highly recommend it! It is fun, easy, and good for our lungs!

Come spin with me, come spin with me, come spin away with me

CF Roundtable – Spring 2013

What I love about Spin is the visualization and the way you can go at your own speed.

Hello CF Roundtable Readers! Hope you are enjoying the spring season that is upon us now. I wanted to share with you, in this issue, my recent experience at Spin class. For those of you who do not know what Spin is, I will explain. It is fancy stationary bicycles that are designed with resistance knobs, handle bars that can be moved up or down, and peddles that hold your feet in so you can stand while riding. They are really cool and they give you a great work out!

With my oxygen (O_2) tank in tow, I set up my bike the other day to start Spin class. Setting up is a process of adjusting the seat, the handle bars and resistance. Along with wiping the bike down with sanitary wipes and then setting up my O_2 tank so it does not fall, Gatorade goes in the drink spot and a towel is kept handy. I have found that just hanging my O_2 tank bag on the handle bars works best for me. I do have a backpack I can put the tank in and I do use that when I am biking outdoors, but I do not like to use it on the Spin bike because the less weight I have to carry on my back, the easier it is to ride. Since the backpack is on your back (hence the name) and the O_2 tanks are not the lightest, whenever I can I use my over-the-shoulder bag. I hang it on the handlebars if that is convenient or sometimes, if I am lucky, it actually fits in the cup holder on the various exercise machines.

Anyhow ... so I am all set up on the bike waiting for class to start. I have my O_2 fitted around my nose, though not turned on yet because I need every bit of O_2 in the tank to do the class. I am still self-conscious sitting there with my O_2 and when I am out in the main gym with it on, too. But I have only gotten positive feedback from people who ask me about it. One piece of feedback I have gotten I will share with you in this story.

The instructor comes in and tells us we will be climbing today. That means lots of resistance on the bike and lots of visualization of climbing a mountain. Climb every mountain, la, lao Okay I digress! LOL! What I love about Spin is the visualization and the way you can go at your own speed. The visualization is wonderful because I can motivate myself by visualizing that I am climbing that mountain and the goal is to get to the top! I'm King of the world! LOL!

I find I visualize a lot in my ways of dealing with CF. I tend to think of happy places when I am going through tough times or tough procedures. I feel the power of visualization is very strong and very healing. I also like that you can Spin at your own speed. This is great for people who are out of shape, have compromised lung function or anything that would limit them in working out. I can peddle the bike at my own speed and put my own resistance and no one knows I am not doing it at the level of the teacher or anyone else. I am doing it at my speed and at my level but still getting a great workout. It really goes with my philosophy of dealing with CF. Some days are better than others and some periods of time are better than others. But I just keep adjusting my sails depending on my circumstances and I do the same at Spin class.

Sometimes my resistance is more, sometimes I peddle faster and sometimes I stand up but, sometimes, I do not do any of that and just peddle in my saddle (sitting on the seat.) All that is okay! I am still out there, I am still doing it and I am still getting a benefit. I feel like in Spin it is not just about how hard you are riding or how fast you are riding, it is about being there and doing it. Like the Nike saying, "Just Do It." So, when I go I just do it to my level and enjoy participating in the class. I have to say, though, that I think I am getting old because I really thought the music last time was quite loud! LOL!

Well, the class was almost over the other day and the instructor was walking up and down the aisles chanting her motivational words of wisdom when she stopped by me and pointed to her nose and asked me, in the middle of class, on her microphone, why I have the oxygen. I thought I would be mortified but, really, it was my chance to say why and then people can move on and not look at me and wonder. Although, I am sure no one was even paying attention. But when something is different about us, I think we all feel self-conscious to some degree, because we all just want to be accepted for who we are. Right!

So, I tell her I have Cystic Fibrosis and only a 40% lung capacity. She says in the microphone how I am her hero and how strong I am - yadda, yadda, yadda. Then the guy next to me starts nodding his head in agreement. I thought I was going to fall off my bike. My feet were fastened into the shoe straps so that would have been impossible. Ha, ha! But, really, I was relieved and now it was not such an elephant in the room.

Again, her reaction was fantastic and it is the third time I have gotten a response like that in the gym. People say how strong I am, but I do not feel that what I am doing is strong. I feel it just is what I have to do to stay healthy.

I tell myself that if one day I have to use the big tanks and roll my O_2 tank into the gym, I will do so. But it is not easy. It is not easy feeling like you are different. It is not easy to feel sad when you are working out because your lung capacity is not what it once was. It is not easy to huff and puff even though you have O_2 cranking in your nose. The workout is still tough on my lungs and I still labor to breathe. It is not easy being green, LOL!

But it is what it is. That is one of my favorite sayings. It seems to really sum up certain situations. I cannot control that I have to use oxygen, but I can control getting my butt off the couch and continuing to work out and be active even though I have had to make adjustments.

That is what life is all about: making adjustments. When you are dealing with an illness that limits you, it is about making the most of what you can do and not about what you cannot do. Are some days better than others? Oh yea! There are some days that I just cannot work out and that is okay. Like the quote in one of my favorite movies, Gone with the Wind, "Tomorrow is another day!" So get out there. Start small and do what you can, not what you can't. Even if it's a two-minute walk to the mailbox, build on that and set small goals. Dealing with CF you will constantly have to start over with your goals because getting an exacerbation really throws a wrench into trying to work out - but that is okay. As Tom Hanks says in the movie Castaway, "Tomorrow the sun will rise and who knows what the tide will bring."

Until next time my friends!

This is dedicated to the one I love
CF Roundtable – Summer 2013

> ***In the end who motivates me and who I do it for is my wonderful husband, Mark.***

Who did not get fazed at all when I first told him I had CF? Who did not flinch when he saw me do my nebs for the first time while we were dating? Who sees me for who I am and not the disease that I have? Who will sleep on a rock-hard bench for two nights in my hospital room? Who will gown up and sit gowned all day in a room that is 8′ x 8′? Who will get blisters on his hands because he wore rubber gloves all day while in that 8′ x 8′ hospital room? Who will gown me up each and every time we walk the halls so I can get the okay to leave the hospital?

Who works all day and then goes to the gym and then comes home to make dinner because I am not feeling well? Who sends me inspirational quotes because he knows I love them? Who will act silly with me when that is not his demeanor? Who lifts me up on a pedestal so high? Who loves me dearly and I know it every day?

Who always gives me the choice of where we should go eat or what we should do over the weekend? Who knows just how to pack all the necessary variety of drinks I need when we go to the beach, in case I get a low blood sugar?

Who takes my neb pieces out of the steamer so they can dry when I am too tired to do so? Then takes the extra step to blow air out of the neb so no water settles at the bottom? Who makes me feel gorgeous? Who loves me so deeply? Who would walk through fire for me? Who has been married to me for almost 16 years now?

Who always thinks of the bright side of each obstacle I have encountered? Who will do manual CPT when I need it? Who continues to sleep in the same bed with me even though I am up coughing all night and he has to get up in the morning for work? Who will always get up from what he is doing if I ask him to do something for me? Who makes sure we do not stay out too late because I still have to do my "medicine?"

Who is so caring? Who is so hot? Who is so generous? Who is so charitable not only to CF but to other great causes out there too? Who motivates me? Who is why I do what I can do to stay healthy? Who makes my heart swell when he walks into the room?

Who motivates me you ask? Three words: My husband, Mark! Mark is why I do it all Mark is why I want to be around till I am old and gray! Mark is my everything!

While my husband, Mark, is my rock and it is he who motivates me and who I do it for, it is still up to me to get it done. It is up to me to do all the treatments, doctor appointments, antibiotics, go through all the pain and do all the therapies. The little voice I hear in my head all day long giving me pep talks is what motivates me.

I think it is very important not only to have a reason to fight and to have people in your life who can motivate you but, most importantly, I feel that the most predominant cheerleader with the loudest voice needs to be you!

In the dead of the night when I am up coughing or I am up scared about what my future holds, it is the voice inside of me that is the loudest and biggest motivator. Sometimes it is screaming, "Move on and let's fight this tooth and nail," but sometimes it is saying, "I am tired and scared to fight this beast we call CF."

I constantly talk to myself all day long with mostly positive pep talks. I have noticed these talks have been more abundant since the downfall of my health over the last two-and-a-half years. For instance, I was just in the gym the other day and I had not been in there for over a week, because I was not feeling well. So, needless to say, it was a very hard workout for me. I was weight training and I was so tired of doing it, but I said to myself, "Come on girl, you got one more machine to do and then you are DONE." I feel it is comical to talk to myself and I find I am doing it A LOT, but it is what keeps me going. I also do pray, which is a whole other topic of discussion for another column.

In the end who motivates me and who I do it for is my wonderful husband, Mark. With his help and my little voice in my head I know I will be able to tackle all that comes my way.

I would like to leave y'all with this beautiful verse from 1 Corinthians 13: 4, which pretty much says a lot of what my Mark means to me and what he does for me on a daily basis. "Love is patient, love is kind. It does not envy, it does not boast, it is not proud. It is not rude, it is not self-seeking, it is not angered, it keeps no record of wrongs. Love does not delight in evil but rejoices with the truth. IT ALWAYS PROTECTS, ALWAYS TRUSTS, ALWAYS HOPES, ALWAYS PERSEVERES."

Love to you, my husband, and thanks for the motivation!

Through my eyes
CF Roundtable – Winter 2014

Hello, CF Roundtable readers! It has been way too long. I have been going through my own personal challenges the last five months, but I am back to writing my column. While I have been down for the count I have watched a lot of movies. I have been on IVs for the last six months and have most likely seven or more months to go.

I know you are probably thinking, whaaaat? I know I am thinking that and I am living it. I have never been on IVs longer than three weeks in my 41 years, and that was only one or two times. So, to think I have doing it for the last six months is mind boggling, but I am getting through it.

I am fighting a bacterium called Mycobacterium abscessus (M. abscessus) and let me tell you this bacterium is relentless! My doctor tells me it can be eradicated, so I am hoping I am one of the lucky ones who shows this bacterium the door!

As I stated earlier, I have been watching a lot of movies and one in particular called "The Curious Case of Benjamin Button," starring Brad Pitt, has struck a chord with me. What struck that chord in particular is a quote that Brad Pitt's character, Benjamin, says to another character in the story, whose name is escaping me. (I am supposed to be writing about "Memory Problems" for this issue so there you go – there is an example of my forgetfulness. LOL!) Anyway, Brad Pitt is asked what it is like growing younger and his response is, "I don't know, I'm always looking out my own eyes."

I thought that was profound in the aspect of relating to CF too. I do not know what it is like to be healthy, to breathe freely, to not struggle day in and day out and for me that is my norm. I am always breathing through my own lungs, doing my therapies, and most importantly adjusting my sails to all the ups and downs of this disease. I adjust so much and all the time that I think I do not even realize how hard my life is or how unhealthy I might be. I just do and I just am. I am just looking through my own eyes and to me this is my norm – to fight, to adjust and to keep moving forward.

Then I thought to myself, what makes some people able to gather up strength and keep persevering even though they are getting kicked every step of the way and others are crippled by their circumstance? As I think about this, I am not really sure why some people can handle adversity and others just crumble. I think it is a conscious choice to keep putting one foot in front of the other. I also feel one needs positive people around them, cheering them on and helping them along the way. As I stated in previous columns my husband is my positive ray of sunshine, for sure. I also think it has a lot to do with what one of my favorite preachers, Joyce Meyer, has said, "Circumstances can't dictate the way you live; you must be stable in all circumstances good and bad." I think that is a great point and what I try to do in my Life. The CF journey has lots of bad times but that does not mean I have to be a sour, pessimistic, and angry person. I feel being that way will not change the circumstances so what is the point?

The last three years my strength and perseverance have been tested. I have gone from an FEV1 of 65% to as low as 31%, lost 17 pounds, had a port placed in my chest, IV infusions daily and have to use O_2 when exercising. It has been an absolute roller coaster. The last six months were my lowest in FEV1 and weight and I feared that this was the beginning of the end. I actually, for the first time in my life, was scared CF was killing me and the road to transplant or death was coming over the horizon.

Did you know the definition of horizon is just the apparent intersection of the earth and sky as seen by the observer? Therefore, the horizon is subjective and can keep moving based on the observer. With that said, during the bleakest of times the horizon is up to you. It can be close and be a signal for positive change or you can see it as being far, far away and there is still time for everything to turn around. Never give up!

My M. abscessus journey has led me to getting a port. I really had no choice in the matter because I was going to have to do IVs for 12 to 18 months and it would be easier with a port then a PICC line. So, I got my port and because I am so skinny you really can see it in my chest and the catheter going up my neck. But it has worked out really well and it is super easy to do Ns and my arms are free. Getting a port was emotional for me because it was again the road to thinking I was declining rapidly. I was becoming the skinny, port in chest, O_2 toting CFer and I just never viewed myself that way nor thought that I would ever get to that point. That was not me! I am not that kind of CF person.

Yet again, I had to adjust my sails. But let me tell you what a number it does on your psyche having a port with tubing hanging from your chest and O₂ tubes in your nose while you are trying to work out at the gym. It has been hard to go to gym in that state, but I need the gym and I will never stop going. I sometimes think with all my para- phernalia hanging off me and my huffing, puffing and coughing someone might be thinking, please girl just go home and rest! But I hope they are thinking what a strong woman and really I am trying to not even care what they are thinking.

I once read that you would be surprised how much people around you are not thinking or paying any atten- tion to you at all. I have really learned to not care what people think and to not let others keep me from being healthy and moving forward. If you think about it, why let someone keep you from doing what is right and what is fun and what is good for your health? Who cares what others think? It's all about what you need to do to get healthier! So, strap those shoes on and get out there. Know that small steps are better than no steps at all.

I leave you with this great quote that Jerry Cahill posted on Facebook by an unknown:

I can choose to let it Define me Confine me Refine me Outshine me Or I can choose to Move on and leave it Behind me

Till next time, CF Roundtable readers, I gotta go to the gym before my next IV infusion!

Buck up, Buttercup
CF Roundtable – Spring 2014

Talking to loved ones really helps me not keep all this fear and sadness inside.

Hello CF Roundtable readers! Hope this issue finds you all doing the best you can do. The topic today is "Maintaining Mental Health." What a doozy this topic is when dealing with CF or any terminal illness.

I would like to open up with a quote from Eleanor Roosevelt that I found to be so appropriate for this column's topic. "You gain strength, courage and confidence by every experience in which you really stop to look fear in the face. You are able to say to yourself, I have lived through this horror. I can take the next thing that comes along. You must do the thing you cannot do." I thought this was so appropriate in my walk, our walk, with CF.

CF is always about rolling with the punches and constantly rebuilding your physical self back up along with your mental self. I am constantly giving myself pep talks along with rebuilding my physicality at the gym every single day. CF has knocked me down so many times and one of my worst moments was recently fighting back from mycobacterium abscessus.

I am proud to say I have come back from the dark, but boy did it take a toll on my physical and mental health. What I like to do to keep myself in fighter mode is to talk it out with loved ones, talk it out with God, listen to music and read very inspiring quotes/songs/poems. I am sure those of you who have been following my column have come to realize I get a lot out of inspiring quotes. These quotes really speak to my soul, and I am able to refer to them, concentrate on them and memorize them to give me strength when I need it.

I keep a quote book, which is a spiral notebook of quotes, sayings, and songs that I find really lift me up and that I can use to lift others up who have their own mental and health battles. A good quote really fires me up and makes me feel positive about what I am dealing with in terms of my health and my life. Here is one that I have put on a postcard from an unknown author, and this quote has really helped me:

I am bigger than this I am not my struggles I will survive this & overcome it I will keep moving forward Nothing will keep me down I am a survivor I will rebuild myself stronger than before. Watch me.

I am sure many of you out there can relate to that! We are constantly rebuilding our minds and our bodies as we fight and come back from our various exacerbations! And praise GOD and our hard effort that we do come back!!!

Music is just food for the soul. There is nothing like a good song to lift your spirits and give you strength. When I was going through seven months of IVs recently, I found a lot of comfort in listening to music during my evening dose as I lay in bed. I was just so very sick, and lying there with the comfort of my music on my Pandora really got me through those evenings. I find it amazing how music speaks to my soul. It can make me cry, it can make me laugh, and it can make me want to get up and fight, fight, fight!

One of my favorite songs that really fires me up is from Sugarland and is called "Stand Back Up." When I hear it I think of myself singing it to my CF. It starts off by saying "go ahead and take your best shot/Let it rip give it all you got/ I'm laid out on the floor but I have been here before/ I may stumble, yeah I might fall." The chorus is "but I will stand back up/ you'll know just the moment when I had enough/ Sometimes I am afraid and I don't feel that tough/ But I'll stand back up!" Booo Yaaaah! I will stand back up and I will get through whatever CF sends my way!

I also talk to God to maintain my mental health. I pray and I have an ongoing dialogue with the man upstairs, and I find the relationship helps me get through the tough times. It's not all pretty, my conversations. Sometimes I am yelling at Him and asking where the heck He is, and then sometimes I am humble and thankful for what I do have in my life.

Finally, talking to loved ones really helps me not keep all this fear and sadness inside. We all need to get it out and sometimes we all just need a hug. A quote from the Sookie Stackhouse books really sums up what it means to talk to, rely on and lean on people to get you through tough times. That character said, "Worries shared are worries halved." I feel it is important to let people in and to not be a hard, stubborn shell. Nobody said the life of terminal illness is easy, and why should we have to do it all on our own? Gloria Vanderbilt once said, "We are not put on this earth to see through one another but to see one another through." I am blessed to have a husband whom I can truly lean on, and I am so thankful that I also have my parents and my mother-in-law along with my husband's side of the family who all see me through!

Well, these are some of the ways I maintain my mental health. It is not always easy and I am not always super upbeat about my situation. I do allow myself to feel dark and depressed if I need it, but I do not let it stay for long. I believe dealing with the hard things in life is easier and more pleasant believing there is a silver lining somewhere in the midst of it all. That is a quote from me! Until next time readers! Stay strong!

Keep on keeping on
CF Roundtable – Summer 2014

> **What everyone is learning now with CF people living longer is that the disease is a full-system attack on all parts of our bodies and all functions of our bodies.**

Hello CF Roundtable readers! Hope this issue finds you all doing well and getting ready to enjoy the summer. I know those of you up North could really use some warm sunshine on your face! The topic for this issue is: "Dealing with Conditions That Are Part of CF." The running joke in my house is that, if something is hurting, not going right, or whatever, it's CF related! But the not-so-funny thing is that it probably is truly CF-related. What everyone is learning now with CF people living longer is that the disease is a full-system attack on all parts of our bodies and all functions of our bodies.

When I was first diagnosed at the age of two, CF was all about the lungs and pancreas. Now we have problems like CF-related diabetes, arthritis, GERD, and many other complications. I often wonder how many different conditions I can handle all at once! I am sure if you have been following my column, you know I am the type of person who says, "Bring it, I can take it!" Although I am a positive person, it is not easy living with CF or, as I tell my husband, it is not easy "being green!" Thank you, Kermit the Frog, for that one!

The two problems that I am currently dealing with are my CF-related diabetes, also known as CFRD, and low lung function. Low lung function is not really a condition or another disease from CF but just a problem that occurs due to the nature of the disease as it progresses throughout my body.

CFRD has been challenging to say the least. I was diagnosed in 2005 and I have to say it is such a high maintenance problem to have on top of the CF I am constantly checking blood sugars, loading up on carbs before doing something physical, carrying around juice packs etc. The difficulty with CFRD is when you are an active person, as I am, blood sugar is constantly being challenged. To make things easier for me, I always have juice packs on me, in case I have a low blood sugar event. I think I need to buy stock in Capri Sun soon! But when that sugar drops, you cannot fool around and you have to treat the low immediately. So, you will always find me with juice packs in every purse, bag or cooler. I guess the good part to having CFRD is I can always bring drinks and granola bars into stadiums or airplanes due to having diabetes. But all in all, I do the best I can to keep my HgbAlc at a good level. I test my sugars constantly and try to do the best that I can. That is really all you can expect from yourself, do the best you can given the situation you are facing.

Low lung function is plaguing me and I am not a happy camper! In four years, I have dropped from an FEV1 of 65% to a steady 38-41%. Let me tell you it has not been easy going through this downturn and trying to live with a low lung function. I now use oxygen when I work out at the gym and, yes, I still go there to work out even though it is so very hard. I am out of breath doing even just menial things. But, as like to say, it is what it is.

I notice for the first time in my life that I look at others running and I am envious. I am envious of those who can walk around the block and not be overly out of breath. I am envious of people at the gym who are working out really hard and doing these great moves for cardiovascular, but I cannot do those. Think kettlebell swings! I have been active my whole life. I have played tennis, baseball, run on the treadmill, taken spin classes and swum. And now it is a different story for me due to the inability to breathe.

I have also been a swimmer my whole life. I have never been scared of the water because I always knew what a strong swimmer I was. But for the first time recently I actually got scared I was going to drown. I started to swim out to a sand bar. About six breast strokes in, I could not breathe at all even though I was taking huge rapid and deep breaths. So, I turned around and was just focused on getting to where I could stand. Well, I made it and I have never been that out of breath in my life! I guess a lung function of 38% does not allow one to swim. So, I learned the hard way. It was very scary and very sad because I no longer can swim. The girl who grew up swimming all summer long, the girl who could jump from a boat and swim around, the girl who snorkeled in Aruba and Hawaii. No longer am I a swimmer. Do they make adult water wings? LOL!

It is easy to give up being active when it is so difficult to be active. I actually feel better during the day when I do not work out. But with that said, I will NEVER give up my work- outs and my activities. I have just made A LOT of adjustments. I wear my Oz when I go the gym and I even leave it on a little longer when I am done, to give my lungs time to recoup. It seems to be helping me to not feel so tired or feel sick at the end of the day, when I leave my Oz on longer after working out. For now, that is my new method to get through my workouts.

As far as other activities, I have had to just modify. I have my husband park the car closer to where I'm going, have him go get the car when we are out, or use my O_2 if I know I will be active outside the formality of the gym. I know working out is so good for your lungs, and I feel small steps are better than no steps at all I believe just moving, no matter how intense or not, is the key.

I believe in consistency; consistency in working out and not so much how hard the work out is but that I am consistent in doing something four or five times a week. Really, all I can do at this point is to adjust those sails and go with the flow. This is how I handle the low lung function. I keep moving and doing the best I can for each day. It is not about how hard you work out but how consistent you are in getting out and moving and doing something. That is just my opinion.

I have also come to realize that I cannot compare myself to others who have CF. Everybody has different lung function, severity of symptoms and other conditions that arise due to CF. So, don't compare yourself to others, just set goals that YOU can achieve. Use other people's ways of doing things to motivate you to do the best that you can in YOUR life and YOUR situation.

I leave you with this quote from Tom Cruise in Vanilla Sky, "Every passing minute is another chance to turn it all around." Get out there and keep turning it all around with each passing day, with each passing minute!

Get back up
CF Roundtable – Spring 2015

Hello CF Roundtable readers! Hope all of you have been doing well and had a great holiday season! Today I wanted to write about a quote from ESPN announcer, Stuart Scott, who lost his battle to cancer recently and passed away. Mr. Scott said, "When you die, it does not mean that you lose to cancer. You beat cancer by how you live, why you live, and in the manner in which you live." When I heard this quote it really resonated with me. Obviously, I substituted CF for cancer and, with that, it really had a lot of meaning for me. CF is a tough walk, I always say, and everyone's walk is unique. CF also has no rhyme or reason to why things go downhill or why things suddenly improve. It is a mysterious and unrelenting beast that I fight daily and even more so as my health has been declining in recent year. But how true it is what Mr. Scott said about coping and living with a terminal disease. It is all about how, why and in what manner you look the devil in the eye and persevere with all the odds against you. I think it would be easy to walk around pissed off, in a bad mood and generally being unpleasant when you are fighting for your life each-and-every day with each-and-every breath. But what good would that do? It doesn't make you feel better. It doesn't get rid of CF. All it does is poison your body, mind, spirit, and those around you. And who wants that? I sure don't and I have never lived my life that way. I have always tried to find the silver lining in the midst of the dark clouds. By doing this, it makes for a more fulfilling and loving life with what life we have left. I think having CF or any terminal disease makes it hard to keep moving forward sometimes. I feel we sometimes judge ourselves based on what we think we should be doing or feeling. Or we see others doing better and we think to ourselves, well why am I not doing well? I am taking all my meds and doing my treatments. I am being compliant. Why am I not seeing the same good results? Well, that is just it. We cannot compare.

We cannot compare ourselves to others or to who we once were. I am constantly comparing myself to how I was when my FEV1 was 65% and I expect sometimes to feel that same way now, but how could I at 29%? It is just not possible and that is okay. There is a quote from John Wooden, who said, "Don't measure yourself by what you have accomplished, but what you should have accomplished with your ability." Wow! That hits the nail on the head. To be present in your current circumstances and to expect out of yourself what you CAN do with WHAT you have going now. For instance, I am still going to the gym to work out even though it is incredibly hard and I need O₂ in order to move these days. But the thing is, I am going. I may not be able to do it as hard as I used to or as often. But I am still going and doing the best I can with what I've got. I have accomplished a lot with my current, and I stress current, ability!

It all goes back to how, why, and the manner in which we live with CF. You gotta keep moving forward with a smile on your face, no matter how much you want to frown. This quote came from an unknown source, "Life has knocked me down a few times ... It has shown me things I never wanted to see ... I have experienced sadness and failures ... But one thing for sure ... I ALWAYS get back up!" Get back up my fibros and cysters! Get back up!

Be an example for all those to see. Be the light that stays on even in the darkest of moments. Keep fighting your CF battle with a light heart, a smile on your face and a spark in your eye. This will feed your soul and spirit and give you strength to battle on. Lastly, I leave you with this quote of Henry David Thoreau, "Things do not change, we change."

Until next time readers!

While I breathe I have hope

CF Roundtable – Summer 2015

Nobody /mows when his or her time is up. That is why it is so important to just live for each day.

I will never forget the words coming out of my doctor's mouth back in February 2015. I was there for a regular CF clinic appointment and knew my health was bad and had been bad for several years now. I fought back from myco-bacterium abscessus, but M. abscessus and living with a progressive disease has taken its toll. My doctor said, "It is time to start the listing process and get listed for a double lung transplant."

I am very grateful my husband was with me that day. You see, he has been coming with me now to CF clinic. Every time I go to clinic these last few years it has been nothing but decline in lung function and to me that is bad news. Well, this time the news was that I needed a double lung transplant. As I heard these words being spoken and transplant coordinators starting to enter the room, I just started to cry. What a thing to hear when you're not expecting it at that moment. When you are thinking to yourself, "I am gonna come back from all this. I am going to increase my lung function. I am going to get off oxygen and I am going to beat this!" I have always beaten CF. I have been fighting for 43 years and I was not gonna stop now. As the coordinators came strolling in and Kleenex boxes were being passed around to me, the harsh reality of what was going to lie ahead of me was scary, daunting, unknown and defeating.

My lung function has been nosediving pretty badly for three years now and I am now at 25 percent. I am 43 years old living with a progressive disease and need new lungs. Growing up, I never thought I would be somebody who was going to need a transplant. It wasn't even on my radar. I have been compliant my whole life and active my whole life. Transplant was not going to happen to me. I never even thought about it. Until now. Now it is at the forefront of my mind-waiting for that phone to ring. Waiting for my second chance. Waiting for my miracle.

The first step in this journey is a three-day evaluation. It is three full days of tests starting from early morning to late in the day. Nothing hurts-it is just an exhausting experience. There is a lot of waiting around. A lot of walking all over the hospital. However, I did use a wheelchair part of the day. I used it mainly due to the fact that my blood sugar was low – I was fasting for a test and the procedure was at the other end of the hospital. If I had walked I would have bottomed out for sure. So, I happily accepted being pushed in the wheelchair, giving my body a chance to rest and lower my oxygen needs.

I got through the evaluation and then it was time for the report to go to a Medical Review Board for review. I got denied. Wait ... what? The concern was the mycobacterium I had a couple years back. Is it really gone because if not it can cause major issues and deathly consequences if it is still in my system. I was told it would eat through healthy lungs. So now I was dealing with the possibility of not being able to get a transplant. A transplant that was going save my life. An idea that I was still trying to wrap my head around and that I really needed right now. Here I am fighting in my head going back and forth in my brain thinking: "Do I really need this now? I can live in this state of health, right? I am not THAT bad, right?" As I am playing the game in my head trying to accept my fate, I am now being told I might not even have the chance to come to terms with needing a transplant.

The next step was a sputum culture tested at the DNA level to see if the mycobacterium abscessus was truly gone. Praise GOD, the test came back negative! No mycobacterium.

The Medical Review Board went over my case again and I am now approved for transplant. Doctors feel confident the M. abscessus does not lurk in my body anymore. However, it is not absolute and there will be special protocol put in place for when I go through the transplant surgery to wash out my lung cavity of any bacteria.

This was now in the month of March or April of 2015 and I needed to get some vaccines before I could get on the actual transplant list. (You cannot have a live vaccine in your body when transplanted.) Now I had to wait the recommended time period for the vaccines to "wear off" (so to speak) to get listed. I am happy to say I am listed as of June 9, 2015!!!

The emotional roller coaster that has been going on since being told I needed a transplant has had its ups and downs. It is so scary to know you need a transplant. I wrestled a lot with trying to believe it truly was time. Which is kind of crazy because I was on oxygen and my lung function was struggling to stay in the low 30s. But I just kept thinking I can live in this state of health. I'd rather struggle and live. At least I will still be living rather than take the chance of transplant and I could die. But what I was denying to myself was the fact that I am dying. I cannot live in the state of health that I am in for many more years. But I can live for many, many years with new lungs. I have a chance with new lungs. I have no chance with my current lungs. But it is hard to see that through the emotions and tears, because transplant is scary. It can have grave consequences. But as I say that, the funny part is, at the rate I am going I have grave consequences. I do not have a chance right now to live many, many years. But I do have a chance with a double lung transplant. But it has taken me a few months to see the light.

The minute I was told I needed a transplant, I created a spiral notebook. I decorated it with uplifting quotes. Imagine that, quotes. If you have followed my column, I am the queen of quotes and they really help me lift my spirits. The biggest fear I have had is being scared of not having enough time. Not living long. It has been very hard to imagine that at 43 years old this could be it. I am not ready to go. What has helped me manage this fear is a quote I have come up with myself. I just keep saying to myself,

"It is about each day, the years will take care of themselves." Look, nobody knows when his or her time is up. That is why it is so important to just live for each day. To be thankful that you have this moment, this time, this day. I feel it also takes a lot of pressure off when you're only focusing on the now. Tomorrow will take care of itself and it will come. But all I can do right now is live in the moment. Cherish the moments I have with my husband, family, and friends. When you really, I mean really embrace and accept living for the present, it truly takes away the fear and pressure of what the future holds.

Another quote that I have come up with that is helping me is, "While there are options, there is hope. Where there is hope, there is life." The option of being able to be a recipient of new lungs is phenomenal. I am actually going to have the chance to live many years. To live breathing! I do not know what it is like to breathe. To breathe like a "healthy" person. It is kind of exciting that I will be able to feel what it is like to breathe! I am very much looking forward to that. It is funny how involuntary breathing is. I think we take it for granted. I never noticed my breathing when showering. Or getting dressed or making my bed. Now, each movement, each activity triggers me to be out of breath. Activities that I have not even thought twice about now have me out of breath. I am amazed how this can be. But my new lungs are going to allow me to breathe again. To breathe better than I have ever breathed in my life. Just the thought of that is a miracle. A miracle I will live and witness for myself. A miracle that a donor family will give me. What a gift!

As I wait for the phone to ring. I continue to work through my emotions of what this journey is going to be for me. At times, I get very, very scared. But at other times I am a little excited. And through this journey I have had family and friends supporting me every step of the way and I cannot thank them enough. How do you say thank you for all the love and support during such an emotional time?

Lastly, I dedicate this to my husband. For if not for him, I would not fight this hard. I would not make it through this journey. He is my light in the dark, he is my EVERYTHING. I dedicate this final quote to him, "To the world you may be but one, but to one you are the world." Mark, you are my world. You are my life. Thank you for loving me! I can truly say I have lived a complete life because I had you! My husband, my love.

The emotional roller coaster that has been going on since being told I needed a transplant has had its ups and downs.

Emergency exits are to the right and left – Ding!

CF Roundtable – Autumn 2015

Waiting for the call to come for new lungs, waiting for life to begin again, waiting for a second chance, waiting and waiting ...

I have settled into my seat. It is a tight squeeze, but I am little so I can clear it. I wipe down anything that I would touch and get ready for the long plane ride to my destination. As we land I am anxious to get off the plane and I can see the gate on the horizon. I am almost there! I can see it! I am so excited! I actually have a lot of emotions whirling around inside of me and these feelings make themselves known at all hours of the day. Wait, the plane has stopped but why!? I can see the gate we are just about there, just a few more feet to go! Then the flight attendant comes on the speaker and says there has been a delay. Please be patient and we will taxi to the gate as soon as we can and you will be on your way to your next destination. Well, that is frustrating. I can see where I need to go, but I have to wait patiently to get there. Ding, goes the sound telling me I can take my seatbelt off, but I cannot get off the plane, the gate is not ready for me yet. So, I will wait in my seat as patiently as I can and dream of what is on the other side of that gate ...

As I have been waiting to get the call for new lungs, I thought how similar it is to waiting on the tarmac when stuck in a plane. How similar it is to see the gate (my new lungs) and to know it is right there and you can walk there faster than it would take for this airplane to get the all-clear to taxi to the gate. Waiting for the call to come for new lungs, waiting for life to begin again, waiting for a second chance, waiting and waiting ...

So, you ask me or wonder how is it I wait? How is it I go on in a state of health that is so very hard to endure? A simple shower leaves me out of breath, and let's not even talk about stairs. Stairs are my nemesis. I am so out of breath from walking upstairs, it is exhausting. I am so tired of being out of breath. But this is my cross to bear, this is my life right now and I will endure until that phone rings with the miracle of more life. Until my "gate" is ready, I will wait in a holding pattern for the phone to ring.

Some of the things that I do to endure this waiting period are to get out to the gym, stay social with my friends, keep smiling and laughing, think positively, and continue to feel God changing me so I can endure what is coming my way! Don't get me wrong, I have my moments. They come at night, usually, when I am getting ready to try to go sleep. Or moments when I am at the gym working out and very much in my own world with my ear buds in and the sounds of music and oxygen flowing into my nose. It is not easy to keep up with life and activities when all you want to do is rest on the couch, when you are tired of coughing and gasping for air. It is quite amazing how hard life can be when you cannot breathe.

Getting out to the gym has been a real challenge for me. It is just so hard to work out when you cannot breathe. I am also very hard on myself and feel like what I do at the gym is pathetic compared to how I used to work out. But I am not what I used to be. I am a 43-yearold, with 28% lung function, on the transplant list. Even being in the gym is an accomplishment. So, with that I do the best that I can when I am there, which includes lifting weights and walking on the treadmill. I am preparing my body for the fight of my life. I am in training! Eye of the tiger! For those of you in my same position just do the best that you can. If that means you got out of bed today and did 12 bicep curls with a can of corn, then so be it! Do not judge yourself on what you can't do, reward yourself on what you can do today. I say today because each day is different. I can feel good one day and not so much the next. So, go with the flow and do what you can. Every little bit matters and is a good job well done!

Maintaining my relationships with my friends has been very important to me. It really makes me feel good to be around them even though I am not feeling well.

Even though after being with them I get in the car and cough out what seems like a gallon of brown glue. But they put a smile on my face and heart and I love them all dearly! Also, my dear friends whom I unfortunately do not see in person but talk with on the phone and text with – I love them dearly! You know who you all are, wink, wink. It is important to maintain those relationships because being alone in your house all day, alone with your thoughts all day, can create a lot of tunnel vision and depression. If you cannot make it out, have your friends come to you. I am very blessed that my friends plan their time around how I feel. I call the shots as to what we are doing, based on how I feel. I am a lucky, lucky girl.

Thinking positively is another aspect of coping with waiting for the phone to ring. I really have to give my husband props for that. He is so positive and supportive that he helps me to be positive. Things I do to stay positive are read positive quotes, watch movies that I love, stay connected with my friends and think about all the awesome things I am going to be able to do when I get my new lungs. It has also helped to talk to some post-transplant people who are doing well, have had good experiences and are positive fighters themselves. I am not saying that I am sticking my head in the sand by talking only with people who have had a positive experience; but I have chosen to be picky about whom I speak to about the transplant. I know things can go wrong, but everyone is different and I choose to speak to like-minded individuals who are positive about their lives and how they approach their disease in general. My husband, as I have stated before, is a real positive light for me. I like to say I am optimistic with a pinch of pessimism. But my hubby looks at the bright side of all problems or issues and that attitude has helped me tremendously. Sometimes the best way to describe a situation is to just say, "You know what, it is what it is." That quote I use A LOT!

Lastly, I really feel God is preparing me for this journey. When I was first told I needed a transplant, it was a very hard reality to accept. Yes, I was on oxygen, and yes, my lung function was low, but I felt I could live this way. In reality, at age 43, living on 24-hour oxygen, not being able to walk up the stairs or take a shower without being overly out of breath even with O_2 and many, many more hardships are just not normal. I think we as CF people tend to really accept our limitations and live with them and build a life around them. Our "normal" really is not normal at all. So, I have found it hard to realize my normal is far from it. God has shown in me this acceptance of needing a lung transplant. He has helped me come to terms and be able to say, "Okay, I am ready. Let the phone ring and let's do this," because I have a lot more living to do! He has brought people into my life in person, via e-mail and via Facebook who have shown me such support and prayers that I get tears in my eyes just thinking of it all. God is by my side and preparing my path - a path to greatness and freedom: freedom from being trapped in my body like I am right now, freedom to do good while I have this time on earth, freedom to be with my loved ones, freedom to just make dinner at night or grocery shop, freedom for the little things in life.

Heading to transplant is a journey. It requires patience, stamina, courage, support, laughter, and love. I look forward to getting back to the simple things in life that we take for granted. No more being out of breath taking a shower, going up a flight of stairs and walking around in the supermarket. The simple things like making dinner and having the energy to do more than one activity during the day and have it even last more than two hours. I look forward to being able to sleep. The little things I look forward to and I will experience all the big things in life too!

I am waiting on the tarmac, I am waiting for the call. I can see it. I can visualize my recovery and fight to get back to what will be the new me! The gate or I should say my lungs are right there and I can just see it. But I will be patient. I will settle into my life that I have now and I will wait for the miraculous phone call. Ding!

Columnist And
Former Director Of USACFA —
Jennifer Hale

January 29, 1972 - December 5, 2015

Jennifer Hale, who was a USACFA Director in 2012 and 2013, wrote what she knew. In her CF Roundtable column, she discussed what she went through living with cystic fibrosis. She wrote of good times and those that were more difficult and recently she wrote of waiting for her transplant. She shared what she did for exercise as well as going through a Nissen Fundoplication surgery. All through her time as a columnist, she was always positive and uplifting with a humor that was distinctly Jennifer.

That she was adventurous and loved life was obvious from reading her quarterly column, "Coughing With A Smile." When she came up with that name, we discussed artwork for it. It was her idea to use a mask and to draw a smile on it because, even though she coughed and at times struggled, she still found humor in life.

While having low lung function, Jennifer wrote of still going to the gym and doing what she could and of trying paddle boarding as a new exercise. When she was younger, Jennifer played softball, tennis and golf - things she had hoped she could once again do after her lung transplant. And she shared with our readers her journey on the road to a lung transplant. How she would wait and be patient. Sadly, she didn't receive the call that would give her new lungs. She died December 5, 2015, at the age of 43.

She shared her spiritual side with quotes that helped get her through the rough patches. But mostly, it was her husband of 18 years, Mark, who really made her life shine. He was her cheerleader when she was not feeling great or was supportive when she had to start thinking of having a lung transplant. She cherished Mark and her good friends for always being there for her. She will be missed by all who knew her.

73468902R00125

Made in the USA
Lexington, KY
09 December 2017